Human-Canine Behavior Connection

Building Better Relationships Through Dog Training

By

Marissa Martino, CTC, CPDT-KA

ISBN-10: 1537070401
ISBN-13: 978-1537070407

DEDICATION

I dedicate this book to my wonderful, loving dog Sully. He has been patient throughout our relationship as I have made mistakes and fumbled through our process. I am lucky to have his presence in my life and for all the gifts and life lessons he has afforded me.

OUR COMMUNITY

Share your transformational journey with us through our social media channels. Use hashtag #PawsAndReward to follow the rest of the community!

Website: pawsandreward.com
Facebook: facebook.com/PawsAndReward
Instagram: instagram.com/pawsandreward

Check out my **Ignite Talk** on this topic:
bit.ly/marissamartinoignitetalk

CONTENTS

ACKNOWLEDGMENTS

My dog Sully, my partner Scott and his children, my mom, dad and sister, all my dear friends and colleagues.

My editors: Brooke, Kristie, Kayla, and Mara.

My original therapist and all my teachers and healers throughout my journey.

All my places of employment: the Humane Society of Boulder Valley, East Bay SPCA and the Dumb Friends League.

All my clients and their canine companions.

And, last but certainly not least, every single dog that has entered my life.

TRAINING DISCLAIMER

This book is designed for you to gain awareness and insight as well as develop your own training plan. The information in this book does not offer a training guarantee. All behavior concerns would be best addressed in person with a positive reinforcement dog trainer specializing in the behavior problem you are experiencing.

To search for a trainer in your area visit:
apdt.com
iaabc.org
ccpdt.org

Introduction

The fall air is crisp and refreshing. The bright sun warms her hand as she wraps a scarf around her neck. She smiles and laughs at her partner as he walks down the street. Gazing into his brown eyes, she remembers the moment she fell in love with him. He is being his usual goofy self, saying hello to everyone in his path. The pair stops to savor the moment in stillness, leaning into one another for warmth and comfort. They smile at each other in adoration. At this moment, the girl realizes just how full her life can be when she is present and ready to receive the gifts of relationship. The moment of silence is broken as he barks in excitement! She follows his bark with an exuberant "Let's Go!" and they race down the street together, hand in hand or should I say hand in leash!

Relationships are all around us. We have relationships with ourselves, our family, our careers, our emotions and of course our canine companions. Here is the story of my many relationships and how I came to develop my training and behavior modification approach, **Human-Canine Behavior Connection (HCBC).**

In 2007, I left my corporate job to attend the Academy for Dog Trainers in San Francisco, California. Not a bad place to spend a few months while studying dog behavior and positive reinforcement training techniques! It was the best time of my life. I woke up each day to the sound of trolleys, the view of the Golden Gate bridge through my window and a surge of excitement to get to the San Francisco SPCA animal shelter. I was young, excited to pursue this dream and ready for the challenges that lay ahead. Courage and I had formed a relationship and I was thrilled to see what we could do together. After completing the program, I was offered a job at the Humane Society of Boulder Valley in the behavior and training department. Boulder, Colorado?! But I had just started my relationship with San Francisco! I was heartbroken that I had to move; however, Courage and I packed our bags, trusting that fate had bigger plans for us. Boy, were we in for a surprise!

I started my job in Boulder and absolutely loved it. It felt wonderful to be a part of something bigger than myself and to give back to the animals that needed it most. During this time, I developed a deep relationship with my Career and vowed to always be of service. At work from 9-5 I was smiling, excited to learn and enthusiastic. However, as soon as I stepped out of the shelter, feelings of loneliness and emptiness descended. What had I done? Why was I here? Marissa, meet Depression. This was not a relationship I was ready for. It was the first time that distracting or busying myself didn't make me feel better and that frightened me. I couldn't stand the pain so I decided to go to therapy to "fix" myself.

Naturally, therapy was uncomfortable. Instead of learning from the discomfort, I decided to blame Boulder...for everything! It was Boulder's fault that my life didn't feel or look "perfect," and boy was I mad at her. My therapist suggested I take responsibility for my happiness. Was she kidding me!? I felt so much resistance towards this process. I never asked for this painfully aware state of mind, and unfortunately, there was no turning back. This part scared me the most. Who was I, now that I had developed a relationship with Anxiety? And who would I become?

One day my therapist asked me a question I will never forget. I was struggling during a session, very upset that I had "allowed" regression in my behavior and thoughts. Gently she asked, "What would you say to your dog training client if she and her dog had regressed in their training plan?" I was shocked when she asked the question and even more shocked as I answered it. "I would say, regression is a part of learning. It's a necessary part of the training process." Wow! If I could channel the compassion and wisdom I had for my clients and their animals when I was speaking to myself, my perspective might shift.

At this point, my relationship with Compassion was in its infancy. But as I delved deeper, I began to notice amazing similarities between the work with my clients and my personal growth journey. The parallels were evident everywhere I looked, providing new learning opportunities daily. This realization softened my resistance to the process of self-discovery. I accepted some hard truths and came to understand that I had been waiting for happiness to knock on my door, all the while ignoring the gifts that life had given me. I'd been focused on what I did not have, where I was not "perfect," and on my mistakes. How could I possibly have experienced any peace? It was from this expanded awareness that Compassion and I developed a deeper and more personal relationship.

While my relationship with myself grew stronger, there was one relationship that was missing from my life. I did not have a dog. People thought I was nuts. They would ask, "How can you work at an animal shelter and not have a dog?!" It was simple. Pets were not allowed where I lived. And then I moved. It was time.

After weeks of searching for the perfect dog, in walked Sully. A six-month-old black lab mix. Sully had a curly tail, long legs for days, brown soulful eyes and a white patch of hair on his chest. There he was, my dog! I was so happy to have found my perfect companion and even more excited to begin our perfect relationship.

As Sully grew both older and more attached to me, he became less tolerant of other dogs. I will never forget the first time he barked and lunged at another dog while on leash. I froze. In that instant, all of my dog training skills were ripped from my consciousness. I remained frozen as he continued to bark and lunge from the end of his leash. Marissa, wake up! Do something! I finally snapped out of it, interrupted Sully's response, and moved him away from the other dog to help him relax. As I sat in the park processing what happened, I chalked it up to him having an off day.

Weeks went by and Sully continued to bark and lunge at other dogs. The heavy realization that my perfect dog did not exist was so sad for me. I was upset with myself for not preventing the behavior, upset with Sully for engaging this way, and embarrassed about the situation since it wasn't what I wanted or expected from our perfect relationship.

It was this moment when I realized that I was still pressuring myself to be perfect. And even worse, I was projecting that onto my dog! I started wondering what else I might be projecting onto Sully? Could his reactive behavior have anything to do with my anxious behavior? This was the moment I realized that my relationship with Sully could be a healing opportunity. Awareness of our interactions would enable me to look deep within myself and see how I operate in all areas of my life and my various relationships.

Let's revisit the beginning of this chapter. The girl is still, sharing a loving moment with her dog, and appreciating what is instead of what should be. This is who I aspire to be every day. With Sully, with myself, and in all of my relationships. It has taken therapy, coaching, life experiences, my friends, family, and especially Sully to help me get to where I am today. I still make mistakes at times. However, I have come to discover that the work is not about making life and relationships perfect; rather, it's about accepting and loving ourselves even when we make mistakes and doing the same for others, including our dogs.

How to use this book

You may have landed here for a variety of reasons. It could be that you're interested in helping your dog through a behavior concern, or that you'd like to expand your relationship with your dog. Maybe you're curious to learn about how the dog training process can help you grow as a person. No matter what your motivation is, I am grateful you chose this book, and I can't wait for your journey ahead.

For a long time, and unfortunately still today, dog training has been positioned or marketed as "fixing" the dog. The pet parent hires a dog trainer and wants them to get rid of the problematic behavior. This is the same approach I took when I hired my therapist to "fix" my depression. There are several problems with this approach, one being that behavior is fluid and no one can guarantee that behavior will always or never be present. However, the biggest concern I see with this approach is that when we state the dog needs to be fixed, we are also making the dog wrong or broken. If we look at the dog through this lens, we run the risk of engaging in relationship damaging behaviors such as blaming and punishing. This approach leaves no room for us to be aware, compassionate and take responsibility for our part in the behavior patterns.

The goal of this book and my training approach is to steer you clear of this automatic way of thinking and to ask you to lean into curiosity and compassion for both you and your canine. This approach is so important to me since we as humans have a tendency to engage in this automatic, defensive behavior in all relationships. By engaging this way, we rob ourselves and others of the intimacy and connection we're longing for.

My training and behavior modification approach is called Human-Canine Behavior Connection (HCBC). The approach consists of 4 steps:

STEP 1: Training the Pet Parent

- Understanding your dog's behavior and their relationship to the world.
- Understanding what your dog is communicating.

STEP 2: Training the Dog

- Implementing management strategies to support your dog's behavior.
- Introducing training & behavior modification techniques.

STEP 3: Enhancing the Relationship

- Understanding your response to your dog's behavior.
- Introducing relationship-building principles to enhance your training and connection.

During my career, I have been witness to many people learning about themselves and expanding as individuals through the behavior modification process and the relationship with their dog. It's uncommon for people to think of dog training as an opportunity for personal development; however, the relationship with your dog is the perfect, safe space to start navigating who you are in all relationships. This leads me to my last step.

STEP 4: Enhancing Yourself

- Learning who you are in all relationships.
- Using the behavior modification process and relationship-building principles to grow as a person.

Our relationship with our canine companions can be a window into how we relate to the world around us. It gives us insight into what holds us back and shows us where we can expand and connect in our own lives.

Going through this process with your dog can be a mirror for you to see how you show up in other areas of your life. Do you get easily frustrated, embarrassed, angry or scared? Can you commit to important tasks in your life? Are you clear on how to identify what you need and how to support yourself when life gets hard? When working with my clients, pet parents get curious, gain internal awareness and draw parallels for themselves, thus creating the opportunity for personal growth and development.

Chapters

Throughout the book and with each presenting topic, I draw parallels for you to not only learn about your dog but also, yourself! As you learn about your best friend, I invite you to get curious about how the information relates to you.

STEP 1: Training You

- Chapter 1: How Dogs Learn - Understanding your dog's reaction to his or her world.

- Chapter 2: Noticing Triggers - Identifying triggers that may upset you and your dog.

- Chapter 3: Identifying Thresholds - Discussing what to do when you both go over emotional threshold.

- Chapter 4: Understanding Canine Communication - Teaching you to read your dog's body language.

STEP 2: Training the Dog

- Chapter 5: Setting Goals for Success - Getting specific about desired outcomes, setting realistic expectations, and making a commitment to the training process.

- Chapter 6: The Training Approach - Introducing the Humane Hierarchy to create safe learning opportunities for your dog.

- Chapter 7: Positive Training Techniques - Introducing evidence-based, scientific techniques used to modify behavior.

STEP 3: Enhancing the Relationship

- Chapter 8: Introducing the Six Relationship-Building Principles

  - Curiosity: Developing personal awareness and curiosity about your dog's perspective to cultivate empathy and compassion.

  - Acceptance: Accepting everything about your dog, including behavioral concerns.

  - Compassionate Communication: Identifying the limiting beliefs used when communicating about your dog.

  - Support & Co-creation: Balancing the needs and desires of both parties in this relationship.

  - Trust: Depositing more positive experiences than negative to maintain a healthy foundation.

- Celebration: Helping you to see the wins, no matter how small!

STEP 4: Enhancing Yourself

- Conclusion - Drawing parallels from the concepts in this book and implementing them in other areas of your life.

Exercises in this book

The exercises in this book are designed to help you develop a personalized training plan to address your dog's behavior concerns. The exercises feature questions specific to you, your dog, and the context in which an undesired behavior is exhibited so that you can develop your situation-specific plan. Make sure to have a journal or notebook with you while reading this book to capture your findings.

Additional exercises will invite you to look closely at the relationship with your dog. Some of what might show up during this process may be worth celebrating and some of it might be challenging to acknowledge. For example, you might realize that you are providing your dog with the appropriate amount of daily physical and mental stimulation, which is worth celebrating. However, you might also discover that you become easily frustrated when your dog barks at the front window. Through this awareness, you realize that your frustration causes you to react poorly during that situation which only causes additional stress for you and the dog.

This process requires you to be vulnerable, which at times can feel uncomfortable. Vulnerability is defined as the quality or state of being exposed to the possibility of being attacked or harmed, either physically or emotionally. Sounds fun, right? Hear me out.

Brené Brown, Ph.D. LMSW is a research professor that has devoted her life to studying constructs such as shame, vulnerability, and courage. These are powerful emotions that we all experience. In her most recent work she interviewed 215 women and discovered that when her participants experienced shame around an issue where vulnerability exists but is not acknowledged, they were often flooded with overwhelming emotions and were unclear about the cause of their reaction (Brown, 2006).

These findings support the importance of personal awareness. When we examine our vulnerable side, we develop a better understanding of ourselves. This awareness provides us the opportunity to take responsibility for our emotional experiences. This is critical to our wellness as well as our surrounding relationships, including the one with our dog!

◆ Get curious with your dog

Before we begin, I'd like you to practice celebration, one of the six core relationship-building principles I will introduce in this book. Take the time to gush about your dog. Please answer the following questions:

- What are five qualities, behaviors, or quirks that make your dog unique?
- What is your favorite memory with your dog?
- How do you express your love and appreciation to your dog?
- Is this relationship a priority?

Introduction References:

- Brown, B. (2006). Shame Resilience Theory: A Grounded Theory Study on Women and Shame. *Families in society: the journal of contemporary human services,* 87(1):43-52.

CHAPTER 1
How Dogs Learn

Understanding how your dog learns and interacts with their world is one of the kindest gifts you can offer your best friend. Even better than a bully stick, I promise! This awareness allows you to see the world from your canine's perspective, offer them the benefit of the doubt and deepen your connection. Plus its super fascinating stuff! Most of my clients report that this newfound understanding has not only helped them address a presenting behavior concern but it has also supported their relationship in ways they did not think were imaginable.

What contributes to your dog's behavior?

Nature a.k.a. Genetics

The age-old question: Nature vs. nurture? Nature refers to the dog's genetic makeup, outlining a dog's physical appearance and behavioral tendencies. Nurture refers to the dog's life experiences and learning history. Most clients want to be able to pinpoint whether their dog's behavior concern is a result of nature vs. nature. Was it learned? Did he have a negative experience? Was he born this way? The answer is always both, it's just hard to determine exactly what percentage genetics plays a role vs. life experiences.

To simplify a very complex topic, it's safe to say that genes matter as they influence a dog's behavior (Martin & Martin, 2011). It's also important to consider that every dog is an individual or a study of one. People make many assumptions about a dog's behavior, based on their breed. Even though these assumptions may seem correct, it can be a slippery slope to solely rely on genetics or breed tendencies to provide us with the full behavioral picture. If we look at our dogs through this lens we might make additional assumptions about what they can and cannot do and that can be detrimental to the training process.

Developmental periods & socialization

Dogs go through a variety of social, emotional, and developmental phases, each of which plays an important role. The socialization period is a critical period of development. The best available data we have indicates this period is from birth to 14-16 weeks old and can vary depending on the dog's breed. It is important to safely expose puppies to a variety of stimuli, including people, places, animals, and children during this time frame (Martin & Martin, 2011; Lord, 2017).

Throughout the process, it is imperative that you go at the puppy's pace in order to achieve positive associations. The best way to do this is to watch your puppy's body language to determine whether or not they feel comfortable in the setting. We will cover canine body language in chapter four of this book. If the puppy does not feel comfortable about the situation, we run the risk of creating negative associations that can impact the puppy's socialization process.

Many pet parents, like myself, were not present for their dog's socialization period for various reasons, most obvious, acquiring the dog after that timeframe. When a dog reacts fearful, anxious or even threatening towards a stimulus or situation a lot of people jump to the conclusion that the dog was abused. That could be the case; however, it could also be that the dog is under-socialized, not having had the proper socialization experiences.

Learning history

The environment plays a huge role in your dog's behavior by reinforcing and punishing specific responses thus creating a learning history. Unfortunately, common cultural phrases such as "dogs are here to please" and "dogs love unconditionally", have us believe that we make up the dog's entire environment. I am here to burst the ego bubble and suggest that we are only just a part of it!

Our dogs are learning all the time whether we are participating in the process or not. Your dog, like many dogs, might bark at the mail person approaching the house. If the intention behind this behavior is to create space away from the mail person and he leaves to deliver mail next door, then the environment (mail person leaving) reinforced your dog's barking behavior.

All behavior has a function.

So in other words, the barking behavior works for your dog. It has a function or serves a purpose for the learner (dog), even though it can be frustrating to those in earshot. Understanding that your dog's behavior, no matter how frustrating, serves a purpose for the dog is a critical concept to understand before embarking on the training and behavior modification process. Asking your dog to give up a behavior that works for him is a big ask! We are encouraging the dog to make a different choice when they have historical data indicating that their current behavior will do just fine. This is why modifying behavior takes patience, creativity, and consistency.

How dogs learn

One way dogs learn is through the process of operant learning, learning by consequence. When I share this process with my clients, I introduce the acronym: A.B.C. (Antecedent, Behavior, Consequence). This acronym allows pet parents to get curious about their dog's reaction by looking at the whole picture (Friedman, 2001).

- **Antecedent** = Stimuli, events or conditions that cue the dog to perform a behavior.

- **Behavior** = The response from the dog.

- **Consequence** = The response from the environment that takes place after the behavior has occurred. The consequence determines if the dog's behavior increases or decreases.

- **Antecedent** = Mail person pulls up in front of the house.

- **Behavior** = The dog barks.

- **Consequence** = Mail person moves away from the house.

If the dog enjoys the consequence of the mail person moving away from the house, then we would predict an increase of the barking behavior. Operant learning is broken into 4 quadrants (Overall, 1997).

- **Positive Reinforcement:** Adding something pleasant to increase the likelihood of behavior. If you give your dog a treat, toy or attention after he sits, the frequency of this behavior increases.

- **Negative Reinforcement:** Removing something unpleasant to increase the likelihood of behavior. An example of this is when you release the tension of the choke chain after your dog sits. Your dog will sit more often to reduce the tension around his neck.

- **Positive Punishment:** Adding something unpleasant to decrease the likelihood of behavior. An example of this is when you leash correct your dog for jumping on another person. If your dog does not like that tension and jerking of the leash, his jumping up behavior decreases.

- **Negative Punishment:** Removing something pleasant to decrease the likelihood of behavior. For example, when your dog jumps up, you remove yourself and the anticipated attention your dog desires; therefore, the jumping up behavior decreases.

	Positive Reinforcement	Negative Reinforcement
If our goal is to **INCREASE** behavior we could:	Add something pleasant	Remove something unpleasant
Example:	Provide a treat for behavior we like	Release the pressure of the choke chain

	Positive Punishment	Negative Punishment
If our goal is to **DECREASE** behavior we could:	Add something unpleasant	Remove something pleasant
Example:	Add a leash correction	Remove our attention from the dog

Co-creating behavior

We are co-creating behavior responses with our dogs all the time. For example, I ask Sully to lie down and wait while I prepare his meal. He walks toward his bed, lies down and waits patiently. I prepare his meal and then place the food bowl on the ground. I use his release cue to let him know it's time to chow down! He pops up exuberantly and gobbles up his meal. My behavior for asking him to wait for his meal was reinforced since he completed the behavior and his lying down and waiting patiently behavior was reinforced with his meal. We co-created this behavior sequence.

This can get tricky at times when punishment is involved. For example, let's say Sully is barking at another dog. I decide to yell at him to make the behavior stop. It does. My yelling behavior was just reinforced since Sully ceased his barking behavior. When punishment works and unwanted behavior decreases, our punishment behavior is reinforced; therefore, we continue using this technique. There are many challenges with relying on punishment to modify behavior and we will explore this concept in detail in chapter six.

Making associations

Another form of learning is called <u>classical conditioning</u>, learning by association. The dog learns that one event predicts another. This type of learning is not contingent on the dog's behavior; rather, it is a result of associations the dog makes in his environment. For example, the leash predicts walks. If the dog loves to go on walks outside then he will create a positive association to the sight of the leash. When the leash comes out he might run to the door with a loose body and wagging tail. Alternatively, if the dog does not like going for walks, he may develop a negative association to the sight of the leash. He might run and hide with his ears back and tail low. The best way to determine what type of association your dog has made, positive, neutral or negative, is by reading his body language.

Operant learning and classical conditioning are happening in conjunction with one another (Overall, 1997). It's not as if operant learning clocks out for lunch while classical conditioning does it's thing. If I want to modify a fearful dog's behavior from hiding in the back of the crate to approaching me, I could address the situation in a variety of ways.

If I wanted to start off using classical conditioning, I would pair my appearance with yummy hot dogs. The dog might start off by watching the hot dogs hit the floor, then he might eat them, then he might move to get the ones out of reach, and lastly, he might approach me and sniff my hand. In that case, he did not have to do anything to receive the hot dogs, rather, it was my presence that predicted the yummy treats. As I continue to toss hot dogs, his association to my presence becomes more positive. We assume this based on the dog's body language, less tension in his face, mouth is open, softer eyes and approaching to sniff. In this form of learning, we changed the emotional association of the stimulus; therefore, the behavior changed.

If we were to approach this situation using operant learning, I would reward the behavior choices the dog is offering; such as looking in my direction, moving towards me, and sniffing my hand. In this approach, we prioritize changing the dog's behavior. If I made the learning process fun and safe, working under the dog's emotional threshold, then this interaction could help shift the dog's association of me from negative to positive.

So, as I mentioned, both forms of learning are taking place at the same time. Whether you're focused on changing associations (how the dog feels), know that behavior can also change and vice versa.

Now that you understand how dogs learn, let's get curious about your dog's behavior. I have provided you with my answers regarding Sully's behavior before we started training so you have a place to start.

• Do you know anything about your dog's genetic makeup?

  • I adopted Sully from a shelter when he was 6 months old; therefore, I do not know anything about his parents.

• Describe your dog's socialization experiences. Were they Positive? Negative?

  • I adopted Sully at 6 months old and missed his socialization window. However, I did safely socialize him to other people, places, and dogs, on and off-leash. Many of those experiences were positive.

• Fill out the ABC's below for your dog:

  • Antecedent = A dog suddenly appears in the environment.

  • Behavior = Sully pulls and barks.

  • Consequence = The dog moves away from Sully.

  • Prediction = I predict that Sully will continue to pull and bark at the sight of other dogs.

• What are some positive associations your dog has made? How do you know?

  • The sound of the food bowl = meal time! He runs to the kitchen with a loose body and a wagging tail.

- What are some negative associations your dog has made? How do you know?

    - The sight of the brush = grooming. His body becomes still, his ears go back and he is avoidant of handling.

◆ Get curious with your dog

- Do you know anything about your dog's genetic makeup?

- Describe your dog's socialization experiences. Were they positive or negative?

- Fill out the ABC's below for your dog:

    - Antecedent = stimuli, events or conditions that cue the dog to perform a behavior

    - Behavior = the response from the dog

    - Consequence = the response from the environment that takes place after the behavior has occurred. The consequence determines if the dog's behavior increases or decreases.

- What are some positive associations your dog has made? How do you know?

- What are some negative associations your dog has made? How do you know?

One of the many reasons it's important to understand how canines learn is to help us examine their behavior through a simple explanation, the Principle of Parsimony, instead of an elaborate story of assumptions. Many of my clients share really creative stories about the intentions behind their dog's behavior. After listening to them, I ask them to share the observations that have led them to make these conclusions. This helps us tease out the facts from the assumptions.

I do not blame my clients for making up these elaborate stories. I have been guilty of this response, myself. It's how our brains are set up to function. In the book, *Emotions Are Made*, by Dr. Lisa Feldman Barrett, she explains why our brains are assumption-making machines. Our brain's job is to understand the sense data from the world and from our bodies. Unfortunately for the brain, it only experiences the effects (changes in the body) and is not aware or privy to the cause of the effects. So, the brain has to guess, pulling on previous experiences and piecing them together. These experiences do not have to be directly related to the current experience. They could be similar to another experience in order to keep us safe and prevent unwanted outcomes (Barrett, 2017).

Making assumptions helps our brains and bodies conserve energy. For example, could you imagine if you needed to use brainpower every day to make educated decisions on what to wear to work? Instead, your brain makes assumptions to aid in this decision-making process by observing the dress code on the first day and then you never have to think about it again, until casual Friday. But you see the point!

It's a great skill to have until it's not. We get into trouble when making assumptions about another's intentions, especially if we believe they are intentionally hurtful or spiteful. When we believe our own stories and stop asking questions we run the risk of operating from misinformed information. Remembering how dogs learn and using the ABC model (Antecedent, Behavior, Consequence) will help you look at your dog's behavior objectively.

◆ Get curious with your dog

- What assumptions have you made about your dog's behavior?

- Is there a simpler explanation available?

❈ Get curious with yourself

- What assumptions have you made about others in your life?

- What questions might you have for that person in order to gain additional perspective and clarity?

Chapter 1 References:

- Lord, Kathryn. (2017). Dog vs Wolf Critical Period. Darwin's Ark. Retrieved from: darwinsark.org/dog-vs-wolf-critical-period/

- Martin, Kenneth M., Martin, Debbie (2011) Puppy Start Right. United States of America.

- Friedman, Susan. (2001). The ABCs of Behavior. *Original Flying Machine*, Issue 9: Nov-Dec, 2001.

- Overall, Karen L. (1997) Clinical Behavioral Medicine for Small Animals. St. Louis, Missouri: Mosby, Inc.

- Principle of Parsimony: Merriam-Webster.com. Merriam-Webster, 2019. Web. 18 Oct 2019.

- Barrett, L. F. (2017) How emotions are made: The secret life of the brain. Boston, MA: Houghton Mifflin Harcourt.

CHAPTER 2
Noticing Triggers

I wake up early to the sun on my face. Feeling good this morning, I decided to head to yoga. After class I get ready for work, refreshed from my practice and smiling as I look forward to the latte I'll order at my favorite coffee shop. But things don't go quite as planned. As the barista hands me my drink, I accidentally spill it all over myself. Ugh! I react. I get upset, grab some napkins, and pat my pants dry. I order a new coffee, shake off my frustration, and head into work. Not too bad.

On the other hand...
I wake up late. I know I need to get to work for an important meeting, and I'm tired after having pushed the snooze button a few too many times. I rush to get dressed then head to the coffee shop to grab a "pick me up" before the meeting. And...I spill the latte on my pants! YIKES - look out! In this instance, I am not operating from a neutral baseline. I am operating from a place of stress. Too many triggers have piled up for me to recover as quickly and elegantly as I did in the first situation. I get upset that my morning is off to such a rotten start and carry the mood with me into the meeting and the rest of the day.

The dog's perspective
Sully wakes up and enjoys a yummy stuffed Kong for breakfast. He gets his mental workout—with peanut butter to boot—and is feeling great. We go for

a run in our neighborhood, leaving him tired from the physical activity. Almost home, we turn the corner and slam right into another dog. Sully freezes and lets out a low growl before recovering quickly as I ask him to check in with me and continue walking. He does a shake off to relieve his tension and we continue down the street, his body postures returning to neutral.

On the other hand...

Sully wakes up to me feeling rushed and late for a meeting. I take him outside for a quick potty break before I leave the house. As we exit our home, two small dogs across the street begin to bark at him. I am rushing us down the street when we turn the corner and run right into another dog. Sully barks and lunges at the dog. It's hard for him to refocus. Fortunately, the pet parent and the dog walk briskly past us giving us the space we need to recover. Sully stops barking but still remains tense as we walk back home.

In the first situation, Sully is more mentally and physically prepared for a hard situation to take place in comparison to the second situation where he is rushed, stressed and there are too many dogs present for him to recover quickly.

Trigger stacking is when multiple stress evoking stimuli are present (Stewart, 2016). These examples are illustrative of the fact that this takes place for both us and our dogs. Knowing the environmental triggers that upset your dog is critical for everyone's success.

Same trigger, different contexts

Not all triggers are created equal. The context in which the dog experiences the trigger plays a huge role in their reaction.

I am walking Sully on a leash when he spots a large dog across the street. The other dog is not paying attention to Sully, sniffing the bushes and checking in with their handler. Sully briefly watches the dog and then checks in with me - great work!

In contrast, Sully and I are in my parked car when that same man and his large dog walk down the street. As the dog gets closer to the car, Sully starts barking. The large dog notices Sully's barking behavior and looks at him. The other dog's body gets tense as he approaches the car. Sully barks even louder in response.

One might say that it's the same trigger, a large dog walking past Sully. However, the contexts are not the same, resulting in different reactions. In the second situation, Sully has very little choice to remove himself. He is trapped in the car as the other dog gets closer and closer thus resulting in a very stressful reaction.

Proactivity

Getting clear about our dog's triggers can help us be proactive rather than reactive when an unexpected situation arises. This knowledge allows us to advocate for our dogs. If a dog has exhibited fearful postures around children in the past, the aware pet parent will now avoid an interaction with a child to prevent unwanted outcomes.

There are many times when people ask if their dog can say hello to Sully while we're walking on leash. Since I know his triggers and want to prevent an unwanted response, I usually use one of these techniques below to maintain positive experiences for everyone involved:

• I cross the street to gain distance away from the other person before they ask for the interaction.

• I start training with Sully which is often a social cue for others to keep their distance.

• I tell them a white lie that Sully is sick and that I do not want to expose their dog. This works like a charm!

Connecting to and naming our triggers is a gift! This allows us to be proactive and manage difficult situations. When I go over threshold and start to feel anxious, my chest clenches up and I feel like I can't breathe. That's when the anxiety comes rolling in and, if I'm not paying attention, I am likely to become reactive myself. I also notice that when Sully goes over threshold, so do I. Sometimes his behavior startles me and I react poorly to his response. This only exacerbates the problem, as my reaction alerts him that something is wrong. In order to help Sully during his behavior modification process, I have made a list of my triggers.

In the next chart I ask myself critical questions:
• Which behavior causes me to react poorly towards Sully?

> • I want to be aware of his triggers so I can be proactive and support him through these interactions.

• Why does this situation trigger me to react poorly?

> • I want to get clear on what is showing up for me emotionally and tease apart the pieces that have nothing to do with Sully. For example, in the chart I state: I feel out of control and embarrassed in front of the other person. I feel inadequate and less than. This projection will affect my reaction which affects Sully's behavior. It is not Sully's responsibility to absorb my emotions, especially when they have a negative impact on him. We are responsible to take care of ourselves in order to thrive in all partnerships.

• What does my reaction look like?

> • I want to be mindful of my reaction to determine whether or not that is the way I want to proceed in our relationship.

• How does Sully react to my behavior?

> • I want to know how my reactions affect Sully and his behavior.

Which behavior causes me to react poorly towards Sully?	Why does this situation trigger me to react poorly?	What does my reaction look like?	How does Sully react to my behavior?
Sully barks at large dogs on leash.	I feel out of control and embarrassed in front of the other person. I feel inadequate and less than.	I get flustered and tighten on the leash.	He tenses up and continues to bark at the other dog.
Sully barks at other dogs from inside the house at the window.	The barking is sharp and startles me which makes me feel uneasy. I do not like feeling uneasy.	I get startled and call his name loudly.	He tenses up and continues to bark at the other dog.
Sully barks and lunges at dogs from inside the car depending on how close they are.	I feel out of control and embarrassed in front of the other person. I feel inadequate and less than.	I get startled and call his name loudly.	He tenses up and continues to bark at the other dog.

It's pretty clear in this chart that my behavioral reaction to "solve" the issue is not helping the situation since Sully continues to bark at the sight of the other dog. If you begin to notice that your reaction is not helping the situation, avoid blaming yourself and learn how to modify your response.

Now that I am clear about my triggers in relation to Sully, I have a few new choices to make in order to support our behavior modification process. I will accept the situation and prevent it from occurring and modify my response which can lead to modifying Sully's behavior.

Which behavior causes me to react poorly towards Sully?	How can I prevent the behavior?	If I cannot prevent it, what can I do to modify my response?	What would be the impact or benefit of this change?
Sully barks at large dogs on leash.	Take less-traveled routes to help avoid run-ins. Bring treats on the walk.	Play a training game with him before he starts to react in order to redirect his focus.	Engaging in a training game helps to keep me calm, giving me something else to do instead of tensing on his leash. My new response ultimately keeps Sully calm too.
Sully barks at other dogs from inside the house at the window.	Close the blinds and give him something to do (food, puzzle, toy) to keep him busy.	Instead of calling his name loudly, I could ask him to do an alternative behavior such as "Go get your toy."	Sully plays with the stuffed toy, helping him focus on something other than the dogs passing by.
Sully barks and lunges at dogs from inside the car depending on how close they are.	Avoid bringing him with me on errands or give him a food puzzle toy to keep him busy while inside the car.	I could calmly ask him to leave the other dog alone and reward him for this new behavior.	Sully learns a new game instead of barking at the dogs walking by.

In each of these scenarios, I have given myself something else to do that will ultimately help Sully have a more positive response to the trigger. It is a win-win for both of us, and it is only possible if I am aware of the triggers—both Sully's and mine.

◆ Get curious with your dog

It's time to get clear about your dog's triggers. Fill out the chart below.

What does your dog react to in a negative way?	What does the reaction look like?	Where does it take place?	What other information is important to note?

How does your dog's reaction trigger you?

Which behavior causes you to react poorly towards your dog?	Why does this situation trigger you to react poorly?	What does your reaction look like?	How does your dog react to your behavior?

How can you change your response in order to help your dog have a better experience?

Which behavior causes you to react poorly towards your dog?	What can you do to prevent the behavior?	If you cannot prevent it, what can you do to modify your response?	What would be the impact or benefit of this change?

✳ Get curious with yourself

Triggers are everywhere—at work, in our relationships, in the coffee shop, with our family members—you name it! In this section, I ask you to identify certain triggers in your life and how you'd like to improve your response.

When do you react negatively in your life?	Why does this situation trigger you to react poorly?	What does your reaction look like?	How does your reaction affect the situation?

Now I invite you to create your own action plan to help you prevent your unwanted reactions as well as engage in new behaviors.

When do you react negatively in your life?	How can you prevent this reaction?	What can you do to modify your response?	What would be the impact or benefit of this change?

Chapter 2 References:

- Stewart, Grisha. (2016) Behavior Adjustment Training 2.0. Wenatchee, Washington: Dogwise Publishing. Print.

CHAPTER 3
Identifying Thresholds

Remember when I was late for work, groggy and rushing to get to an important meeting? I grabbed a latte and, of course, spilled it on my pants. Uh oh - look out! I was about to pass my emotional threshold in 5, 4, 3, 2, 1. Going over threshold is defined as the moment a behavior changes. In the previous example, I went from somewhat agitated to very agitated the moment the coffee spilled on my pants.

There are many different types of thresholds, such as fear thresholds, frustration thresholds, and joy thresholds. I might go from calm to overjoyed when I learn I received a raise. My behavior might change from sitting at my desk, checking email to jumping up and down with a huge grin on my face after receiving the good news.

When there are too many stressful triggers present, we are likely to go over our fear or anxiety threshold. It is at this point we - humans and dogs alike - are more likely to display unwanted or out of control behaviors. Thus, it is essential to identify both triggers and thresholds when entering into the behavior modification process so that we can be preventative and know what to look for.

The brains of dogs and humans respond to stress in a similar way. When we are over threshold, learning shuts down and emotion takes over. The entire process starts in a part of the brain called the amygdala. It activates the sympathetic autonomic nervous system (SANS) and the limbic system. When these systems are activated, the brain goes into fight, flight or freeze mode. This response is meant to help us survive what is perceived to be a threatening situation. During this process, two neurotransmitters, norepinephrine, and epinephrine are released. They stimulate the adrenal glands, which secrete cortisol into the bloodstream. Since we are now on emotional autopilot, our prefrontal cortex is suppressed. Since this is the part of the brain where learning and thinking take place, it explains why dogs cannot respond to cues when they are in distress (Seksel, et. al., 2014).

Dogs are not being stubborn in times of stress. Physiologically they cannot respond!

This is why we cannot solve a math equation while being held at gunpoint. We have bigger fish to fry at that moment! After the stressful situation has passed, the body's stress response is supposed to return back to normal. But these changes do not take place right away, and stress responses can reappear when we don't expect them. You're on a lovely walk with your dog, who is terrified of bikers, when one whizzes past you. Your dog will likely enter flight mode and try to get away from the bike even though he's on a leash. Even after the scary stimulus (the biker) has passed and your dog has done a full body shake off to release some of his tension, he may still be on heightened alert. A few minutes later someone steps out their front door. Your dog balks on leash and refuses to walk with you. His reaction confuses you until you realize that he may be over threshold from the previous experience. It is not about the person at the front door; it's more about his physiological state at that moment.

Training plan

When I start working with my clients, we always train under threshold and away from the triggering context first. If the client wants to reduce the dog's barking behavior when people walk by the house, there is no way we will start the training process at the window during a barking episode. But why not, if that's where the behavior concern takes place? Since that situation evokes an emotional reaction, that is not the best context for the dog to learn a new behavior. In order to be successful, we need to teach him a different response when he is under threshold and able to learn.

It can be a challenge

One of the hardest parts about modifying behavior is keeping the person or dog under threshold so he or she can make new, better choices. This is especially challenging when life gets in the way. If a dog is fearful and lives on a busy street with loads of bikers and pedestrians, it can be hard to control her environment so she is under threshold. It takes creativity and planning. In this case, we could change the time of day we take her for a walk. We could also walk her in a low-traffic neighborhood or cut the walk short. We do our best to control the environment but understand this is not always possible.

Ways to keep your dog under threshold:

- Make sure to meet your dog's needs daily by providing plenty of mental and physical stimulation to keep them relaxed and satiated.

- Choose the right environments for your dog. Make sure they have plenty of space and choice to remove themselves from scary situations.

- Provide visual barriers in order to reduce their exposure to a trigger. This can be as simple as stepping behind a car while you are out walking.

- Take frequent breaks so your dog is not constantly exposed to a trigger.

- Use training games, play, and engagement to refocus your dog to you and away from the trigger.

Learning opportunity

When our dogs go over threshold, we can use that as a learning opportunity. One of my clients wanted to socialize her fearful dog, Cora. When people entered the home, Cora would cower in a corner and remove herself from the visitors. My client did a great job keeping Cora under threshold by inviting one friend over and working with that same person for a series of visits. She told her friend to sit quietly on the couch and ignore Cora. As Cora became a bit less wary, air scenting toward the couch and relaxing her body a bit, my client asked her guest to toss treats from about ten feet away, avoiding any eye contact. The two continued to socialize Cora over the course of a few visits, watching as Cora eventually did a low tail wag and then approached the visitor. By the fifth visit, Cora had warmed up so much that she hopped into the friend's lap for a serious petting session.

So excited by this progress, my client invited several people over to the house in hopes of expanding Cora's social circle even further. My client forgot to have them follow the protocol (ignore Cora, sit on the couch and toss treats). The visitors entered the house and immediately reached for Cora. No surprises here, Cora backed into a corner and started shivering. She was way over threshold.

What did we learn here? It's easy to go over threshold, even when we do not mean to. My client had the best intentions by continuing her dog's socialization. However, she got carried away because Cora was doing so well and assumed the dog would respond positively to all new people. This is a very common mistake for pet parents to make during the training process.

Recovering back to baseline

Deciding to recover from a situation before moving on is a hard choice to make at times. Let's say I am training Sully to ignore other dogs and check in with me, and he is doing great as long as he's at least fifteen feet away from another dog. Feeling confident, I decided to move him closer to the stimulus. When we get eight feet away he starts barking. At that moment I have two options. I can either get upset about his reaction, or I can navigate us away from the oncoming dog in order to get us back to baseline and under emotional threshold.

If I choose the first option, I will be frustrated with Sully for barking and upset with myself for pushing him too far too fast. Even worse, I might project my personal frustration onto him and act out in anger (I can't believe

I did that!), embarrassment (I can't believe other people saw me!), shame (I am a dog trainer for heaven's sake!), or fear (What if he pulls loose?). My emotions might create a negative association and exacerbate his response even further. However, if I choose option two, I can bring us back to a place where we can settle, breathe and recover from the experience. This is obviously the best choice - and sometimes the harder choice - since humans can be just as reactive as dogs. We want the negative behavior to stop immediately, so we react to make it go away instead of accepting and learning from the experience.

◆ Get curious with your dog

Recall the triggers that cause your dog to react poorly from chapter two.

- What is your dog's threshold in relation to the triggers?
    - How close are the triggers to your dog?
    - How many triggers are present?
- What can you do to help your dog stay under threshold during this situation? What helps your dog feel better when he or she is upset?
- How will you recover and get back to baseline if necessary?

Rational?

In the previous example, I share the potential thoughts and feelings racing through my mind while my dog engages in unwanted behavior. These thoughts can be defined as cognitive distortions, exaggerated or irrational thought patterns that have the potential to influence our feelings and behavior. In 1976, psychologist Aaron Beck first proposed the theory behind cognitive distortions and in the 1980s, David Burns was responsible for popularizing it with common names and examples for the distortions. I have listed and defined several below to name a few (Beck, 1976).

- **Jumping to conclusion** = Operating from assumptions about my dog's behavior.
- **Polarized thinking** = Either our dog is perfect or the worst behaved dog

in the neighborhood. This level of thinking does not leave room for anything in between.

- **Blaming** = Not taking responsibility and blaming the dog for everything.
- **Overgeneralization** = Taking one instance, dog barking at the dinner table, and generalizing the thought to be the dog is non-stop barking every minute of the day.
- **Discounting the positive** = Not taking into consideration the positive choices and behaviors the dog is offering.

Getting frustrated and leaning into this way of thinking about our dogs, ourselves and others is going to happen. I encourage you to be more aware of when you start operating from cognitive distortions, pause and get curious about the situation in order to pull yourself out of the automatic thought loop.

✳ Get curious with yourself

- Which cognitive distortions have you operated from in the past?
- How has that impacted your relationship with your dog?
- How has that impacted your relationship with others?

Taking care of ourselves is one of the best ways to take care of our relationships. I know personally, that when I am overwhelmed, overworked and not exercising, I am in no place to create loving and intentional interactions with Sully, my family, and friends. If I start to get impatient with Sully on walks or get frustrated with him during training sessions, those are red flags for me to stop, take a break, support myself and then resume my interactions.

Ways to keep you under threshold

- Exercise! It's a no-brainer that exercise helps keep you balanced and energized.

- Sleep. Getting more sleep helps you feel more mentally, physically, and spiritually refreshed.

- Unplug from the digital world.

- Nutrition. A healthy diet keeps you focused and aware rather than sluggish.

- Schedule downtime, whether it's a yoga class, meditation, knitting or snuggles with your dog.

- Take breaks from the people or situations that bring you down.

- Communicate what you need in order to create healthy boundaries.

- Allow space to experience your emotions.

- Get creative by drawing and making crafts.

- Breathe!

✳ Get curious with yourself

- Where in your life do you wish you had more control over your responses?

- What triggers contribute to you reaching your threshold? Can you prevent them in any way?

- What do you need to do in these situations to keep yourself under threshold?

Chapter 3 References:

- Seksel, Kersti. (2014). Stress and Anxiety - How Do They Impact the Pet?. World Small Animal Veterinary Association World Congress Proceedings. Retrieved from: vin.com/apputil/content/defaultadv1.aspx? pId=12886&catId=57087&id=7054740

- Beck, A. T. (1976). Cognitive therapies and emotional disorders. New York: New American Library.

CHAPTER 4
Understanding Canine Communication

Years ago, when Sully, my family and I relocated to Denver, I was concerned about our living situation. We moved into a boutique, pet-friendly apartment building, which meant we would be running into other dogs in hallways, stairwells, and elevators. Sully and I had never lived in this type of housing before, and I wasn't sure how he would adjust.

After only a few days of living in the new building, Sully had already developed a clear response to his environment. Whenever we stepped into the hallway, he went on high alert: ears perked forward, body tense, lip licking, closed mouth, and a high tail.

Why did he react this way? We had never run into another dog in the hallway, nor could we hear any dogs from inside other units. I'm sure he could smell them, but that didn't seem to warrant his guarded behavior. What had him so stressed? And then it hit me like a ton of bricks...it was me! I had him so stressed.

It was me holding my breath when we entered the hallway. It was me tensing on the leash. It was me talking to him in a stiff, anxious tone. It was me who had single-handedly conditioned him to be stressed in this location. Therefore, it was up to me to desensitize him to the hallway and change his association. Luckily we were only working with three days of negative experiences as opposed to three years!

I put my trainer hat on and made some adjustments:

- Each time I entered the hallway, I took a deep breath and then initiated play with Sully. He loves it when I say, "I am going to get you" and then chase after him. I chose that game so we could get our bodies moving, think about something else, and create a positive association with the location. Whenever we entered the hallway, he looked back at me, and play bowed, waiting in anticipation of his favorite game!

- Outside my apartment door, Sully and I spent five minutes training each day to work on focus behaviors and to help him feel comfortable in the space. We situated ourselves near my door in case another dog entered the hallway and we needed an exit strategy.

- I organized a few of his dog friends to make "guest appearances" in the hallways so he could get used to seeing other dogs in our building. I used his friends so it would be a positive experience for him.

- Finally, Sully always received his favorite treats, such as cheese and boiled chicken, inside the building. I would reward him for checking in, walking next to me and sitting.

Within two weeks, Sully's behavior had changed. The hallway had become a fun and inviting space to enter. We'd developed coping strategies that lowered our stress, changed our behavior and turned the once threatening environment into one of safety and connection.

Learning to listen

If I had not known how to read Sully's subtle body language cues, I may have missed his alert stress reaction in the hallway. By not dealing with it right away, Sully's reaction could have worsened over time, creating a much larger issue down the road.

Whether we are interacting with our friends, family members, or canine companions, it is crucial to be aware of how and what we are communicating. Observing our dog's body language is a mindful practice, asking us to stop and be present. I developed an acronym to teach pet parents how to practice this mindfulness as they observe their dogs. The acronym is W.O.A.A. (Watch, Observe, Assess, Act Accordingly).

Watch - This step is about taking time to observe the dog rather than interacting right away. Often mesmerized by how cute our dogs are, we reach for them without stopping to observe whether or not they want to interact. Most people would not respond well if a stranger were to approach and hug them without any introduction. The same can be said for dogs. Take your time and observe.

Observe - Now that you have spent time watching your dog, state what you see. Be specific, for example, the dog is moving his body away from me, sniffing the ground, ears are back and the tail is tucked. These observations are objective rather than subjective and give much more reliable information than generalized impressions.

Assess - Based on the objective observations, it's time to assess what the dog is feeling. Since she is moving her body away from you, sniffing the ground with her ears back and tail tucked, it's safe to say she appears uncomfortable with the interaction.

Act Accordingly - Your educated assessment of the dog's behavior has helped you determine how she is feeling. Now you can adjust your actions. You decide to turn to your side, kneel down, blink your eyes and allow the dog to approach you. Act accordingly can also include making adjustments to your dog's environment in order to promote healthy interactions with others. If you notice your dog exhibiting displacement behaviors and fearful postures when a friend says hello, give your dog a break from the interaction and then observe her response. Does she reapproach and solicit attention? Or does she stay close to you and avoid the person? Act accordingly to your dog's response.

Always listen

Behavior is fluid and can change all the time depending on the context. You wouldn't meet someone for lunch, check-in with their body language, facial expressions and tone of voice only at the beginning of the outing. Instead, you would consciously or subconsciously check in throughout the entire interaction in hopes to maintain a healthy connection. I encourage you to do the same with your dog. Remember the steps of the W.O.A.A. acronym, watch, observe, assess and act accordingly to ensure your dog is as comfortable as possible during all interactions.

All behavior has a function

When I am teaching pet parents about their dog's body language I encourage them to not only state the body postures and behaviors they are observing but also note the context in which they are taking place. I do this for several reasons. The first is to remind pet parents that all behavior has a function. That function may be to increase or decrease distance been the dog and another stimulus or it could function to express an emotion. For example, a dog might growl to communicate to an oncoming dog that he wants space or another dog might lean against a person's leg to indicate that she wants additional petting.

Not all behavior is created equal

Another reason why I encourage pet parents to notice the context in which the behavior is taking place is because not all behavior is created equal. The context can be a big clue as to how the dog might be feeling at that moment. For example, not all rolling on the back to expose the belly means the dog wants a tummy rub and not all jumping up means the dog wants to lick your face and provide you with a friendly hello.

For example, a pet parent brings her puppy to the local cafe in hopes to socialize her. The puppy is hiding behind the pet parent, body still, ears back and tail is tucked. People walk passed the puppy noting how cute she is, while others ask to say hello. The pet parent ignores the puppy's avoidance behaviors and allows people to approach. As the strangers reach for the puppy, she rolls over to expose her belly with her mouth closed and tail tightly tucked.

A different puppy is playing with her pet parent in the park. She is bouncing around on leash and running in the leaves. Someone stops to say hello and before they can even ask to pet the dog, the puppy has rushed up to the person with a loose body posture and wagging tail. The person starts petting the dog. The dog leans into the person's hands for additional scratches. She rolls over on her back with her mouth open, soft eyes, and a relaxed body.

In these two scenarios, both puppies are rolling over to expose their bellies when meeting new people; however, the behavior has different purposes in each interaction. In the first scenario, the puppy is uncomfortable with the interaction and rolls over to offer an appeasement gesture to cut off any perceived threat. In the second scenario, the puppy has approached the person, leaned into petting and because of her relaxed body postures, we can assume her rolling over is an invitation for a tummy rub.

Behavior is fluid

Fear and aggression co-exist on a spectrum. For example, I could react fearful towards the sight of a spider, trying to remove myself from it, but once it touches my leg, I might escalate towards aggression by swatting at it to go away. There are some dogs that give a lot of warning that they are uncomfortable, such as growling for a prolonged period of time while other dogs may growl for a brief second and then escalate to biting. Below is a list of behaviors and postures to pay attention to (Handelman, 2008).

Threat Response Spectrum: behaviors dogs do when they are feeling threatened by a stimulus, situation.

• Avoidance, look away

• Mouth the hand of the person touching them

• Head whip: looking quickly towards the person or dog

• Freeze

• Bark

• Growl

- Lip lift

- Tooth Display

- Muzzle punch

- Lunge

- Snap

- Bite

Alert & Tense: Everything is Forward, Up

- Body Weight: forward and tense

- Ears: up and forward

- Tail Carriage: held high, may be over back, can be wagging stiffly and quickly

- Eyes: direct stare, eyes appear to be fixated on stimulus

- Mouth: baring teeth, lips are puckered forward or closed

- Piloerection (Hackles): fluffing of hair around shoulders, down the back, and/or on the tail

Fearful Body Postures: Everything is Down, Back

- Body Weight: back

- Ears: down and back, flattened against head

- Tail Carriage: down, may be tucked

- Eyes: looking away

- Mouth: closed, growling

- Piloerection (Hackles): fluffing of hair around shoulders, down the back, and/or on the tail

When I was training Sully to enjoy the hallways in our apartment, there were a few obvious indicators that he was stressed. He took treats from my hand with a hard mouth and his fur was shedding like crazy! Here are some other examples that indicate when a dog is feeling anxious and stressed (Handelman, 2008).

Stress Behaviors - behaviors dogs engage in when they are stressed.

• Taking treats hard when the dog usually takes treats gently

• Not eating treats at all

• Trembling

• Panting

• Sweaty paws

• Pacing

• Whining

• Vocalizations

• Stress lines in face

• Mouth is tight and tense

• Excessive shedding

• Dandruff on coat

Just like humans, dogs have a variety of smaller, more discrete gestures they display before going to the extreme response. The first set of behaviors is displacement behaviors and refers to a dog's way of coping with the environment. These behaviors include shaking off, licking of the lips, scratching, sniffing, stretching, sneezing and yawning. You might read this list and think, "Wait, my dog yawns at night; isn't he just tired?" Or, "My dog shakes off after a bath; isn't he just wet?" The answer is yes. But these behaviors are considered displacement when they happen out of context. For example, your dog walks into the vet's office and he starts scratching all of a sudden. He then begins pacing around the waiting room and suddenly does a shake off. Your dog is not wet, nor does he have a skin allergy. So why is he shaking and scratching? This is his way of calming his nervous system, lowering his stress and dealing with an environment he deems threatening.

I have had many clients say, "He was fine and then suddenly, out of nowhere, he started barking and lunging." After observing their dog's behavior, I usually discover that the dog was not fine; rather, he was doing everything he could to hold it together. During these situations, I often observe a tense dog, exhibiting several displacement behaviors before the escalation.

Displacement Behaviors: behaviors happening out of context, helping the dog cope with the environment (Handelman, 2008).

• Lip Licking

• Licking self

• Scratching

• Sniffing

• Yawning

• Shake Offs: dog is shaking off his whole body as if he just had a bath

• Stretching

• Sneezing

I encourage pet parents to look for these behaviors, paying special attention to when they take place. I've noticed that Sully licks his lips when he meets another dog nose to nose. He also does a shake off right after the greeting. Since I know these are displacement behaviors, I can assume he is mildly stressed while meeting other dogs. This information helps me make the choice to keep my leash greetings very short, so as to avoid a negative experience for my dog and to prevent him from escalating beyond the yellow flags.

Avoidance behaviors make up the second set of yellow flag behaviors, and they are the most easily overlooked. During an initial consult, I had a client ask me why I had not said hello or pet his dog yet. I said, "Because he hasn't indicated to me that he wants me to. Since I have entered your home, he has avoided approaching me and has positioned himself within three feet of my reach." The pet parent ignored my observations and continued to tell me how friendly the dog was and that he wanted me to say hello. I said, "Let's test your theory." I looked in the dog's direction, careful to avoid eye contact, and called his name in a high pitched voice. He looked at me and moved several inches further away from me. Talk about clarity. He already said no, thank you and now he was really saying no, thank you. This was very eye-opening for the pet parent which launched us into a discussion on body language.

Avoidance Behaviors: Behaviors dogs do to indicate they do not want to interact (Handelman, 2008).

• Walking away

• Looking away

• Disengaging

A set of behaviors that are often misinterpreted are called appeasement behaviors. Dogs use these to "cut off" any perceived threat in the environment and to communicate, "I come in peace!" If Dog A approaches Dog B in a confrontational manner, with a stiff body and direct stare, Dog B might respond by looking away, raising a paw and licking his lips. Dog B engages in these appeasement behaviors to indicate to the other dog that he does not want a confrontation (Rugas, 2006).

Humans sometimes misinterpret these as "guilty" responses. People often believe their dog knows not to engage in a specific behavior, such as eating from the garbage, counter surfing or stealing their running shoes. I am not certain what your dog knows or doesn't know since we cannot ask him. What I do know is that your dog is reacting in response to your reaction of getting upset and yelling. At that moment you are the perceived threat, and he is offering appeasement gestures to indicate that he does not want any confrontation. Not to mention that if the garbage incident took place twenty minutes before you got home, he already reinforced himself by licking the peanut butter jar clean!

Appeasement Behaviors: behaviors that dogs offer as a greeting or "cut-off" signal to inhibit perceived aggression in other dogs or people.

• Face licking of a person or another dog

• Paw raises

• Lip retraction/Submissive grin: smiling or showing teeth while maintaining a loose body

• Rolling to expose tummy

• Submissive urination

I encourage you to start looking at your dog's behavior more closely. By noticing these groups of subtle behaviors, you can prevent unwanted, escalated interactions between your dog and others. Use this chart as a reference when reading your dog's communication. For a fully illustrated guide of canine body language, please reference Barbara Handelman's book *Canine Behavior: A Photo Illustrated Handbook*.

	Body	Tail
Distance Increasing	❖ Relaxed body Approach ❖ Weight even on all 4 legs ❖ Leaning in ❖ Jumping up with loose postures ❖ Play bow	❖ Tail wag at neutral height, loose wagging ❖ Tucked tail ❖ Tail even with body
Distance Decreasing	❖ Displacement behaviors ❖ Turning head away ❖ Cower, head low ❖ Tremble ❖ Avoidant ❖ Roll on back ❖ Weight back ❖ Stiff body ❖ Weight forward ❖ Height seeking posture	❖ Tucked tail ❖ Tail down (not tucked) ❖ Tail arched over back ❖ Stiff wag

	Ears	Eyes	Mouth
Distance Increasing	❖ Ears in neutral position	❖ Soft eyes	❖ Closed and relaxed ❖ Open and relaxed
Distance Decreasing	❖ Ears back ❖ Ears forward	❖ Averted ❖ Direct contact ❖ Hard/fixed stare ❖ Wide eyes	❖ Closed and tense ❖ Open and tense ❖ Panting ❖ Head whip ❖ Low tone vocalization, barking, growling ❖ Agonistic Pucker

◆ Get curious with your dog

Choose three different scenarios in which you'd like to observe your dog's body language. Use the acronym W.O.A.A. (Watch. Observe. Assess. Act Accordingly) to determine what your dog is communicating.

Three different scenarios might include:

1. Petting your dog.

2. When guests enter your home.

3. When you take your dog for a walk.

In the first scenario, you might watch your dog and see that he is lip licking, looking away and his body is tense. You realize he is communicating his discomfort with the physical touch, so you "act accordingly" by removing your hands and allowing him space. This exercise will train you to observe your dog's body language, communication, and responses in a variety of settings.

Use the chart below to fill in your responses:

Scenario #1:	Notes:
WATCH	
OBSERVE	
ASSESS	
ACT ACCORDINGLY	

◆ Get curious with your dog

- What were some things you noticed about your dog's reaction to the various stimuli in different scenarios?

- What conclusions might you draw from these observations?

- Did you notice new body postures you hadn't before?

- How does this new information help understand your dog?

Our body language

Roxie is pacing at the front door, which leads Jennifer to believe she needs to go outside for a potty break. Jennifer puts Roxie's harness and leash on and heads out the door. As they walk down the street they listen to the birds and smile at the neighbors. Jennifer has slack in the leash and is calm and collected as she walks through the neighborhood.

Suddenly, Roxie tenses up, her ears forward and hair raised along her back, communicating to Jennifer that another dog must be near. Jennifer tightens the leash, holds her breath and pulls Roxie closer to her. Her intention is to have better control over Roxie; however, this action further escalates Roxie's tension. Roxie, now with limited choice and leash restriction, associates the leash tightening with an oncoming dog. The two confirm for one another that "danger" is up ahead.

When the dog is within ten feet of them, their anxiety explodes. Roxie barks and lunges while Jennifer yells and tells her to stop. After what feels like ten minutes, they safely get past the other dog, and eventually, Roxie stops barking. Jennifer is shaken and tired from holding Roxie back. Roxie does a full body shake off to relieve the tension. The two continue on their walk, cutting it short in order to prevent another negative run-in.

I am exhausted just reading about this scenario! And yet, this is a common leash experience for many pet parents. Jennifer has the best intentions for pulling Roxie close to her; however, this communication further exacerbates the dog's reaction by leaving her with limited choices.

Roxie communicated with her body postures that:

• There is a dog up ahead.

• She has a stiff body, ears forward, hair raised along her back.

Jennifer communicated:

• There is a dog up ahead.

• She is tense, holding her breath and pulling on the leash.

They were both communicating the same thing! Jennifer's body language confirmed for Roxie that the upcoming situation was tense and scary, which made it much more likely that Roxie would associate the situation with fear and anxiety and escalate her behavior.

How could Roxie and Jennifer's communication have resulted in a more positive experience for them both? As soon as she sensed a dog ahead Roxie's body language changed. Her mouth closed, ears perked forward and body stiffened. Noticing this, and not wanting to contribute to Roxie's anxiety, Jennifer could have chosen a different response. Here's another possible outcome.

- Jennifer scans the environment and notices where the other dog is and which direction he is walking.

- She gets happy and excited, saying; "Let's go," which prompts Roxie to follow her. In doing so Jennifer creates additional space between Roxie and the oncoming dog.

- Jennifer plays "Find it" with Roxie by sprinkling an endless amount of treats on the ground.

- Jennifer remains calm and plays this game until the dog is out of sight.

Roxie responds to her attempts by following Jennifer away from the dog and playing the game. Between treats, Roxie periodically checks to see if the other dog is present, but her tension has dissipated and she is comfortable once again.

No lunging, barking or tension.

More positive communication. More positive

associations.

Jennifer's response to the situation dictated how both she and Roxie handled it. We need to remember this in every moment we spend with our dogs. We have the choice to make each interaction a positive one.

◆ Get curious with your dog

Think about your interactions with your dog and whether or not they are supporting or harming your relationship. Here are a few prompts:

- What is your body language communicating to your dog?

- How is your body language supporting your dog's behavior?

- How is your body language detrimental to your dog's behavior?

W.O.A.A.

Our body language and behavior choices not only affect our dogs but also affect the people in our lives. In the last two chapters, we discussed the importance of knowing our triggers and thresholds. I invite you to use the W.O.A.A. acronym to check out what's showing up for you the next time you feel over threshold in other relationships.

W.O.A.A. (Watch, Observe, Assess, Act Accordingly).

• Watch - Take the time to pause and see what is coming up for you before you react towards someone or a situation.

• Observe - State the facts about the situation, your thoughts and any other observations that are present.

• Assess - Based on your observations, determine how you are feeling. Allow space for you to experience those feelings.

• Act Accordingly - Now that you have taken the time to pause and honor your reaction, determine the next best steps, such as, taking more time to evaluate, asking a friend for advice, or prepping yourself to have a hard conversation with yourself or a loved one. Reflect back to others what you might be assuming or thinking.

I have a tendency to want to skip right to the "Act" part in order to resolve conflict. Jumping into that part makes me feel like I am taking action; however, sometimes, it is not the best choice. It has taken me a long time and a lot of practice to slow down, sit with the conflict and then determine my next steps!

Chapter 4 References:

- Handelman, Barbara. (2008) Canine Behavior A Photo Illustrated Handbook. Wenatchee, Washington: Dogwise Publishing.

- Rugas, Turid. (2006) On Talking Terms with Dogs: Calming Signals. Wenatchee, Washington: Dogwise Publishing.

CHAPTER 5
Setting Goals for Success

I have always been one to set a goal and get it done! While this habit is one of my greatest strengths, it can also be my nemesis. Yes, it's what helps me achieve greatness, experience new things and explore the world. But this tenacity also causes me to put unnecessary pressure on myself. I strive for perfection, even though we all know that is impossible. I want this quality to remain a strength, so I am always trying to strike a healthy balance between accomplishing goals and accepting where I am in any given process. I do this by reciting "I am exactly where I am supposed to be" when I sense myself getting overwhelmed and stressed. The ability to find this balance is a crucial component of both behavior modification and personal growth! In this section we will address four fundamental elements that are key to your behavior modification success:

• Defining your goals.

• Prioritizing your goals.

• Identifying their impact.

• Identifying realistic expectations.

Defining your goals

By now you have a better understanding of your dog's behavior and your own emotional response so it is time to determine your training goals. If your goal involves the word "should" then you might want to rethink where that specific goal is coming from.

The use of the word "should" can often indicate that the goal might not be exactly what you want. For example, if your goal is "I should teach my dog not to pull on leash," ask yourself why this is important to you. Walking nicely on leash is definitely a plus as a pet parent; however, do you really care or are you projecting? Would it be okay if you learned to manage this behavior by walking your dog using a no-pull harness? If so, then, by all means, purchase the harness. Stick to what matters to you.

When identifying your goals, think about a day in the life with your dog. Does he always bark at you while you prepare his breakfast? Goal #1: My dog waits patiently for his meal. When you go on walks does he chase after squirrels? Goal #2: My dog ignores distractions and checks in with me. And so on. Your list of goals can be as short or as long as you want, just as long as each one is important to you.

◆ Get curious with your dog

Write down the goals you have for your dog. I want you to really dig in here. Get detailed!

1. What do you want your dog to do instead of the problem behavior?

2. Where would you like your dog to do this new behavior?

3. When would you like your dog to do this new behavior?

4. What distractions will be present?

For example, I would like my dog to (1) walk next to me on my right side while on leash in our (2) neighborhood (3) each day while (4) other people and dogs are present. Write down your goals using the four questions as guidelines.

Prioritizing your goals

I am a realistic trainer and know that not everyone has endless time in the day for training. Since we have very busy lives, I invite you to make the training process realistic by pacing yourself wherever possible. If you have more than one goal, identify which one(s) can be managed right now and which one needs to be addressed right away. Remember to include everyone in your family in the process so the training and communication are consistent.

Things to consider when deciding management vs. training:

• Does this affect you daily? Does your dog pull your arm out during each walk?

• Does it impact your dog's quality of life? Does your dog have separation anxiety when you leave for work?

• Is it dangerous for your dog? Does he dart out the front door? Does he inconsistently come when called?

Identifying the impact

Once you have prioritized your goals, make three columns. Column 1 is the goal, column 2 is the priority level and column 3 is the impact of achieving the goal. Identifying the impact is imperative, as it is your motivation for sticking with the training process.

Goals	Priority	Impact
Goal #1: I want my dog to walk next to me on my right side while on leash in our neighborhood each day while other people and dogs are present.	Higher priority as this affects our life several times a day.	I will enjoy our leash walks more and be motivated to provide additional exercise and socialization for my dog. My dog would then be more relaxed while in our house and avoid engaging in boredom behaviors such as barking and chewing.
Goal #2: I want my dog to wait at the front door even when the door is open and there are distractions outside.	Lower priority as I can train this behavior when I have free time while also managing my dog's access to the front door in order to keep him safe.	My dog will be safe.

◆ Get curious with your dog

Goals	Priority	Impact

Now that your goals are clearly outlined and you understand their positive impact, it's time to explore how you're going to make these goals a reality.

◆ Get curious with your dog

- What is standing in your way of committing to you and your dog? What can you do to adjust that barrier?

- When was the last time you committed to something important in your life? What inspired you to make a commitment?

- Where and how are you consistent in your life? How can you use that consistency with your dog and the training process?

- Who will hold you accountable? When you are having a hard time achieving your goals, how can you help yourself get back on track?

Identifying realistic expectations

One of the first behaviors I taught Sully was to sit for his meal. We practiced this behavior for several days before he aced it. The following week, we approached the front door together for our walk, both of us facing the door instead of facing one another. I asked him to sit using the verbal cue we'd practiced and he just stood there. In his head, I imagined he was saying, "What's the hold-up?! Let's go outside!"

It was at that moment that I remembered, "Oh yeah, dogs do not generalize behaviors from one context to another." Sully had learned how to sit when I was facing him, not when we were standing next to one another. Just the slightest change in the context created confusion for Sully.

This inability to generalize can get in the way of our goals and training plans. We teach our dogs specific behaviors in the house and then expect them to generalize that training game to ALL locations, distractions, and scenarios. This type of learning cannot happen on the fly. The learner needs to rehearse the skills repeatedly in environments that cultivate success. This is the primary reason I encourage you to train your dog in a variety of contexts so she understands the cue and behavioral expectation is the same even if the environment changes. We will discuss this concept in more detail in chapters six and seven.

◆ Get curious with your dog

• Do you have realistic expectations for your dog's behavior? If not, how has that gotten in the way of your relationship?

• How can you reframe your expectations so that you and your dog are successful?

Real-life application

The "sitting" experience with Sully got me thinking about my own challenges in this area. My commitment to speaking my truth with friends and family is a perfect example. I made a vow that whenever I was feeling hurt, offended or needed to clear an assumption with one of my friends, I would explore what I needed to say and then initiate the hard yet rewarding conversation. After months of practicing, making mistakes and developing my voice, I got relatively good at speaking from my heart. However, when it came time to do this behavior in my work life, whoa, look out - deer in headlights! I remember saying to myself, "I thought clear and heartfelt communication was a strength of mine!?"

Just as I was about to get hard on myself it dawned on me: I wasn't generalizing the behavior from one context to the next. It was the same issue

I'd seen with Sully. I decided to make a conscious effort to communicate openly in all contexts, not just with my friends and family. No one steps into the game knowing how to get everything right the first time. We need to practice in a variety of settings before we master a skill.

✳ Get curious with yourself

- Do you have realistic expectations for other relationships in your life? If not, how has that gotten in the way of your relationships?

- How can you reframe your expectations so that your relationships are successful?

CHAPTER 6
The Training Approach

Sniff, Sniff. Oooh, I smell hot dogs - Woohoo!! Sit, shake, down. Bark, bark! Sit, shake, down. *What?!? Why haven't I gotten a hot dog yet?! I am trying ALL my tricks and nothing is working.*

Bark, bark, jump up, bark! *How frustrating!* Scratch, lip lick, yawn.

I think he just asked me to do something, but I haven't heard this word before. What does he mean? Sniff, sniff. Those hot dogs smell good! Sit, shake, scratch, pace.

I don't know what he wants from me! I am going to be stuck here forever. I'll never get another hot dog and will probably starve to death! Just tell me what you want, human!

I am always amazed that dogs figure out what we need and want from them, even though we don't speak the same language. But if dogs did speak our language, I imagine the above scenario would go through their minds multiple times a day.

It is our responsibility, not the dog, to make the training process clear, consistent and possible for the learner (APDT, 2019).

Least intrusive, minimally aversive

Dog training is an unregulated field; therefore, pet parents have many different dog training approaches, philosophies, and techniques to choose from. It's information overload and I often wonder how they make any decisions at all.

To address this issue, several organizations, including the International Association of Animal Behavior Consultants (IAABC), the Certification Council of Professional Dog Trainers (CCPDT) and the Association of Professional Dog Trainers (APDT), published position statements indicating that they support a Least Intrusive, Minimally Aversive (LIMA) approach to dog training and behavior modification.

LIMA describes a trainer or behavior consultant who uses an approach that is least intrusive, minimally aversive to the learner in order to achieve behavior change. In this context, intrusive can be defined as removing control from the learner to varying degrees. Aversive can be defined as using a stimulus that may cause pain, fear, or frustration during the learning process. Adherence to LIMA also requires the behavior consultant to be educated and skilled in animal behavior modification (IAABC, 2018).

When discussing LIMA-based approaches and training plans one often refers to a roadmap called the Humane Hierarchy. The Humane Hierarchy serves to guide professionals in their decision-making process during training and behavior modification (IAABC, 2018). The Humane Hierarchy was first introduced by Dr. Susan Friedman, Ph.D., a psychology professor, and applied behavior analyst.

The roadmap is designed with six "exits" to take along the behavior modification highway. The majority of behavior concerns can be addressed using the first four exits (Friedman, 2018). As I define each "exit", I will walk you through the common behavior concern, jumping up to greet visitors at the door.

Before we try to solve the behavior concern, we must first determine what is the function of the behavior. Let's look at our ABCs.

• Antecedent = People walk into the home.

- Behavior = Dog jumps up.

- Consequence = Guests say hello to the dog.

- Prediction = If the dog likes the consequence of attention, then the jumping up behavior will increase.

The behavior of jumping up can have many different functions depending on the context; however, in this case, we are assuming that the function of the behavior is to receive attention from the guests.

Exit 1: Health, Nutrition, and Physical Setting

Exit one involves having a veterinarian address any possible contributing health concerns and a behavior consultant address any environmental concerns, such as welfare and enrichment. One example might include making sure the dog is not in any pain. If the dog is experiencing discomfort, he could be jumping up or away from the person to avoid the pain reaction.

Exit 2: Antecedent Arrangements

This exit involves rearranging environmental factors or events that may be causing the behavior or making it worse. A few examples include greeting visitors outside the home with the dog on leash in order to reduce the excitement at the front door, asking the guests to reduce their enthusiasm towards the dog as they enter, or placing the dog in another room away from the front door with a yummy food puzzle.

This exit is especially important for both the dog and the pet parent. If the pet parent gets into the behavioral habit of setting up the environment so that it works for the dog, it also works for the person too. Win-win!

Exit 3: Positive Reinforcement

Exit three involves reinforcing the desired behavior in order to increase the probability of that behavioral response. In order to ensure success, these behaviors should be taught out of context before you ask the dog to perform the behavior when visitors enter the home. An example might include teaching the dog to grab a toy, stand, or sit without the presence of guests arriving at the door.

Exit 4: Differential Reinforcement of Alternative Behavior

This exit involves reinforcing the desired behavior while at the same time extinguishing the unwanted behavior. However, if you have done a good job training the behavior out of context and gradually increasing the difficulty, then you should rarely if ever, need to use extinction (in this case, ignoring the dog) as part of this process. For example, now that you taught your dog to grab a toy in a low distraction environment when no one is present, you can start to make the training game a bit more challenging. For example, you could:

• Ring the doorbell and then cue your dog to grab the toy.

• Ring the doorbell, prop the door open without anyone present, and then cue your dog to grab the toy.

• Ring the doorbell, prop the door open with a known person present, and then cue your dog to grab the toy.

• And so on.

Another benefit to this step, since it involves training in context, is the ability to reinforce the new behavior with not only food, or in this case the toy, but also with the social contact, what the dog desired in the first place. Double reinforcement!

Proceed with caution

We should proceed with caution before taking the fifth exit because implementing these techniques can be frustrating for the learner since their previously reinforced behavior no longer works in that context.

Imagine you start your first day of work. You walk in feeling eager and enthusiastic. You meet with your boss to review your assigned tasks. You are excited to learn. Instead of telling you what is expected of you and reinforcing you for getting the behaviors correct, your boss either; ignores your incorrect attempts without any guidance (extinction), removes paid time off from your account when you offer the incorrect behavior (negative punishment) or consistently nags you about your poor performance until you change your behavior (negative reinforcement).

Gosh, that sounds awful right?!? Wouldn't it have been a whole lot clearer and easier if your boss taught you the correct behavior from day one! This is how our dogs must feel when we engage in the techniques below.

Exit 5: Extinction, Negative Punishment, and Negative Reinforcement
Extinction is defined as removing the desired reinforcer from the dog permanently in order to reduce the probability of this behavior occurring in the future. Most people know this technique as ignoring the dog until the unwanted attention-seeking behaviors of barking or jumping up decrease.

Negative Punishment is one of the quadrants of operant learning. It is when one removes something pleasant; therefore, the behavior decreases. In our example of jumping on visitors, this might include having the visitor turn their back or leave the room. If the removal of the person is punishing to the dog we should see jumping decrease.

Negative Reinforcement (escape-avoidance learning) is also one of the quadrants of operant learning. It is when one removes something unpleasant; therefore, the behavior increases. In our example of jumping on visitors, this might include releasing the pressure of a choke chain after the dog stops jumping up and sits down. The behavior of sitting will increase if the dog wants to avoid the tension around their neck.

The last exit

It is advised that if a trainer has reached the sixth exit and the problematic behavior still persists, they should consult with another professional first to ensure they have exhausted all options before taking this exit. In my experience, consulting with other professionals can be a gift. Through collaboration and a fresh set of eyes, we are always able to come up with additional solutions that relate to the previous exits. This helps us avoid the last exit.

Exit 6: Positive Punishment

This exit involves applying an aversive (a stimulus the animal behaves to avoid or escape) after the unwanted behavior occurs in order to reduce the frequency of the behavior. This might include applying a shock, physical pressure or kneeing the dog in the chest after the dog jumps on the visitor.

There are many people and trainers that skip all exits and jump straight to this technique. Even though this technique works in reducing unwanted behaviors, it has some major fallout for the learner (Friedman, 2018).

- Frustration is increased because you are not telling the dog what to do instead.

- The techniques can damage your relationship and change your dog's behavior in a negative way. This may present as fearful body postures and avoidance behaviors, with the potential of escalating to threat displays, such as growling, snapping, biting.

- You run the risk of creating a negative association with something that was not intended. If you pull back on the choke chain every time your dog barks at another dog, she may begin to associate the pressure of that choke chain with the sight of the other dog, not with the barking behavior.

- Sadly, some dogs shut down. They engage in a learning process, called learned helplessness. When an animal's attempts to escape aversive events are blocked they tend to give up trying even when their power to escape is restored. Scientists study this phenomenon in many different species and find that after applying an aversive to the learner (for example, shock) the animal stops moving or "behaving" for fear of the applied aversive (Maier & Selligman, 1976). So to some pet parents, they think they fixed the behavior concern since the dog is no longer reacting poorly but we must ask ourselves about the welfare of that animal. There are better ways to teach the learner what you want.

- It is counterintuitive, yet imperative you avoid punishing your dog's warning signs and communication attempts, such as growling, barking and snapping, to name a few. If you punish your dog for growling, the behavior decreases, which one might consider that successful. However, your dog still feels threatened about the stimulus or scenario that elicited the growl. She may feel even more threatened now that you're upset with her. The next time she encounters this situation she may not growl - having been punished for this response - but instead, try another behavior such as lunging or snapping. Your plan has now backfired! It's not the growling that's the problem, it's the emotion behind it that needs to be addressed.

A kind approach

Now that we have traveled down the Humane Hierarchy highway, I hope you have a better sense of the approach I subscribe to when teaching both my canine and human clients. Dog training is a less formal way of saying applied behavior analysis. We are borrowing the same scientific principles that are studied in humans and applying them to our best friends. That means we learn and interact with our worlds the same way.

Most of my clients realize very quickly that I am training them as much as I am training their dog. If the behavior goal is to modify your dog's barking and lunging on leash, I have to assess your behavior in addition to the dog. Are you tensing up on the leash? Are you yelling at the dog? If your behavior is not supporting the desired outcome, then that means I am modifying both your behavior and the dog's behavior. Good thing for me, the same rules apply.

Change the association, change the behavior

In chapters two and three, I have stressed the importance of training under threshold whenever you can, creating an opportunity for your dog to learn a new way of responding. Desensitization and counterconditioning, two training techniques that work in conjunction with one another, help the dog change both his response and association to a given stimulus.
Desensitization is the process of gradually exposing the animal to a trigger without provoking the stressful response, and counterconditioning teaches your dog that the scary stimulus predicts something positive (Overall, 1997).

The process

If your dog barks and lunges at other people when on leash, training under threshold would include determining the distance you need to be without your dog reacting to the person. If there is no response when you are 30 feet away (on the other side of the street) from an approaching person, start your training process there! Each time your dog looks at the other person, feed him a yummy treat. Repeat this action. By doing this you are communicating that the person on the other side of the street predicts hot dogs rain from the sky!

After you and your dog have repeated this several weeks in a row, you might begin to notice a change in his behavior (he is looking at you instead of the other person). There are two key reasons for this change:

• You were in a space where he could learn (under threshold).

• You changed his association and how he feels about the person, which ultimately changed his behavioral response.

What happens if you feed the dog a treat when he barks?

But...what if the other person gets a bit too close for comfort and your dog starts to bark at the same moment you feed him the treat? Don't fret! You are not rewarding the barking. Wait - what? How does that NOT reward the barking? Simple. Your dog is not barking to get a treat; he is barking to make the other person go away.

Here is another way to think about it. I want to rob a bank. (I don't really, but let's pretend for a moment.) The problem is the large dog that guards the entrance at night. He barks, snarls, and lunges at me when I approach. Hmm - how am I going to get past him? I need to change his association of me. The next time I approach, I toss him a filet mignon. The dog barks and barks and then suddenly stops when a piece of meat lands at his paws. He eats it, all the while growling and barking at me. I continue to visit the bank several days in a row, tossing him huge cuts of meat. Does his barking increase or decrease?

It decreases!

He now associates me with a yummy steak! His association changed, and the behavior followed. Now he wags his tail and licks his chops in anticipation when he sees me. So, rest assured you will not be rewarding your dog's barking when you help him create new associations to threatening stimuli in your environment using food. However, if your dog is barking at you at the dinner table and you decide to share a piece of steak with him from your plate, you are absolutely rewarding the barking. That is a completely different scenario since your dog desires the food at that time.

Start small

As I've stated before, when working with dogs that have a hard time with specific triggers (growling at children, barking and lunging at other dogs), it's important to work under the dog's emotional threshold. When the behavior modification sessions are set up properly, it may seem like your dog's social world is getting smaller. This always confuses my clients as they hired me to "socialize" their dog to the scary stimulus. I understand their desire to expand their dog's social world; however, most of these dogs are not ready for that. They have been tolerating, or worse, reacting poorly to the stimulus, being forced to interact with it over and over again. Their association becomes even more negative, making the situation worse.

My goal is to always create positive experiences for the dog when the stimulus is present. Usually, that involves distance, taking it slow, reading the dog's body language and only moving ahead in the training plan when is the dog is ready. This is one of the most important key concepts in behavior modification.

The opposite of this technique is called flooding, exposing the learner to the fear-eliciting stimulus for an extended period of time (Overall, 1997). If you have a fear of spiders, could you imagine being locked in a closet full of them?! Some dog-specific examples might include:

• Bringing a reactive (barking, lunging) dog to the farmer's market to see if they can "get over it".

• Bringing an under-socialized dog to the dog park and letting him "work it out" with the other dogs.

- Forcing the fearful, squirming puppy to stay in your arms as you cuddle her.

Going at your dog's pace will ensure long-term success. By doing so, you begin to create positive experiences around the scary stimulus, thus making the desired emotional and behavioral shift.

Chapter 6 References:

• International Association of Animal Behavior Consultants. (2019). Hierarchy of Procedures for Humane and Effective Practice. Retrieved from: m.iaabc.org/about/lima/hierarchy.

• Association of Professional Dog Trainers. (2019). Position statement on LIMA.What Do You Want the Animal TO Do?. Retrieved from: apdt.com/wp-content/uploads/2017/01/position-statement-lima.pdf.

• Certification Council of Professional Dog Trainers. (2019). Application of the Humane Hierarchy Position Statement. Retrieved from: www.ccpdt.org/wp-content/uploads/2015/01/Application-of-the-Humane-Hierarchy-Position-Statement.pdf

• Friedman, Susan. (2019). What's Wrong with this Picture? Effectiveness if not Enough. Retrieved from: www.behaviorworks.org/files/articles/What's%20Wrong%20With%20this%20Picture-General.pdf

• Maier, Steven & Selligman, Martin. (1976). Learned Helplessness: Theory and Evidence. *Journal of Experimental Psychology*, 105, 3-46.

• Overall, Karen L. (1997) Clinical Behavioral Medicine for Small Animals. St. Louis, Missouri: Mosby, Inc.

CHAPTER 7
Positive Training Techniques

In chapter six, we covered the training and behavior modification approach. In this chapter, we will discuss the training process for you and your dog. The chapter is broken into four parts:

1. Choosing the right reinforcers for your dog.

2. Introducing training techniques.

3. Teaching your dog life skills.

4. Designing successful training sessions.

Choosing the right reinforcers for your dog

In order for behavior to increase and continue, it must be reinforced. A reinforcer is defined as consequences (stimuli, events or conditions) that cause a behavior to increase in frequency. Primary reinforcers are stimuli we already find reinforcing, such as food and water. Secondary reinforcers are previously neutral stimuli that have been paired with existing reinforcers, such as a marker word or the clicker (Pryor, 1999).

All dogs are individuals. My dog might find carrots reinforcing while your dog turns his nose at this offered treat. At the beginning of the training process, I use food as the reinforcer for a variety of reasons:

- I can get creative with my food choices and use low, medium and high-value options.

- It's easy, fast and simple to deliver a small piece of food to the dog after the desired behavior.

- I can get a lot of behavior repetitions in one training session since it takes little to no time to chew and swallow.

When choosing your dog's food reinforcers please consider:

- Individual Preference: Most pet parents call me and say their dog is not food motivated. If that was truly the case, the dog wouldn't survive. When I arrive at the pet parent's home, I offer their dog a variety of food items and we're training in no time! Variety is the spice of life and your dog is no different. Offer your dog different types of treats and food items to see which one works for them.

- Determine Value: What does my dog like? Love? Go bonkers over? This will determine your hourly rate. I might pay my dog off using kibble ($8.00/hour) when I am asking him for an easy behavior such as sit inside the house, no distractions present. I might pay him off using steak ($20.00/hour) for a more challenging behavior such as a 15-foot recall on trail.

Sometimes reinforcers can be considered too high value when the dog exhibits behaviors that indicate they are having a hard time focusing. They might ignore a cue, get excited and jump up, stare and drool or start offering behaviors with high reinforcement histories (such as sit) to get the yummy piece of liver. In this case, you might want to change your reinforcer from something your dog goes bonkers over to something they like so they can focus on the learning process.

When can I stop carrying treats?
The short answer is never. Stick with me. Keep in mind, that science tells us that in order for a behavior to continue, there must be something in it for the learner, in this case, your dog. My answer to this question consists of two parts:

1. Expensive behavior deserves a large paycheck! Yes, I still carry high-value (pieces of steak) with me on trail with Sully. When I ask him to ignore the great outdoors and check-in with boring old me, I need to have something just as reinforcing for him if I am competing with the smell of fresh fox urine.

2. Incorporate reinforcers throughout your dog's day. Once the dog has learned a cue in a variety of contexts (in the home, yard, on walks, with distractions) I start to incorporate reinforcers other than food to maintain the learned behaviors. These reinforcers are often referred to as life rewards.

Examples of life rewards:

- Hopping in the car
- Sniffing a novel spot outdoors
- Getting the leash on for a walk
- Taking the leash off for a romp
- Access to a pond, lake, creek
- Access to a park
- Access to a trailhead
- Access to a person
- Access to another dog
- Going into the backyard
- Play with pet parents
- Access to toys
- Getting attention

Life rewards are different for every dog. While Sully likes belly rubs (leans into petting with an open, relaxed mouth), he loves going off-leash (his body is loose, tail wagging and jumping up in excitement)! Training is a consistent lifestyle and not a single activity that we do at the beginning of the dog's life.

These reinforcers allow us to make training a part of our daily routines and help us provide variety to the dog. Take a minute to answer the questions below so you have a better idea of what your dog's reinforcers might be.

◆ Get curious with your dog

Food or treats:

• What does my dog like?

• What does my dog love?

• What does my dog go nuts over?

Life rewards:

• What does my dog like?

• What does my dog love?

• What does my dog go nuts over?

Teaching your dog a marker

The marker is defined as a bridge between the behavior performed and the reinforcer delivered. It marks the moment in time when the dog offered the desired behavior. Many people use the words, "good" or "yes" when marking a dog's behavior. I like using the clicker, a small sound device. The clicker is only used during training sessions; therefore, it remains salient to the dog.

To teach your dog what the marker means:

• Say the marker word (or sound the clicker).

• Deliver a yummy treat to your dog.

• Do this 10 times in a row.

• Avoid marking and treating at the same time. You want the sound of the marker to predict a treat is coming.

• If you mark, you must always treat. So, if you do not have a treat, do not say the marker word and instead simply praise your dog for the correct behavior.

How to use a marker

Mark the moment the dog does the behavior correctly. Here is an example:

• Antecedent = I ask my dog to sit using my verbal cue.

• Behavior = The dog sits.

• Consequence = I sound the clicker and deliver a yummy treat.

Introducing training techniques

Shaping

Shaping is the process of clicking and treating small approximations of behavior in order to reach the desired response. If I want to teach my dog to spin in a circle, I will start by clicking and treating when he looks in a specific direction. Once he has mastered that, I will click and treat when he looks and takes a step. Next, I will wait until he takes two steps before I click and treat. I will continue to reward the approximations until I get the full desired response - spinning in a circle.

Capturing

This is one of my favorite ways to train since it teaches us to look for behaviors that we like instead of looking for behaviors that we don't like. Let's face it, as a culture we're really good at pointing out what we do not like. Capturing helps us focus on the positive, click the behaviors we enjoy, and reward the dog handsomely. I click and treat Sully when he chooses to walk next to me or sits at the street corner without me asking. Even though I did not cue it, the behavior still deserves a reward.

SMARTx50

One of my favorite trainers, Kathy Sdao, introduces a concept called SMARTx50. See, Mark, And, Reward Training. This technique invites pet parents to count out 50 pieces of their dog's food and reinforce the choices the dog is already making throughout the day. It not only challenges the pet parents to start noticing how great their dogs are instead of waiting for them to make poor choices but it also incorporates training throughout the day. I love teaching this exercise in my very first session with pet parents, especially if they have a new puppy or newly adopted dog in their home. It's an easy exercise for everyone to play and the more we reinforce behavior, the more it will happen (Sdao, 2012).

Adding a cue

Although we are tempted to teach our dogs verbal cues right away, this is ineffective. Dogs communicate primarily through body language. When teaching a new behavior, one of the techniques I might use is L.A.W. - Lure, Action, Word.

- **Lure**: First, use an enticing treat at the end of your dog's nose to manipulate the rest of his body into the desired position. Where the head goes, the body will follow!

- **Action** (hand signal): Once your dog successfully follows the food lure into the desired position, try using the same hand motion without the food lure in your hand. This motion will become your hand signal for the behavior.

- **Word** (verbal cue): Only when your dog fully understands the hand signal should you introduce the word/cue.

Once your dog is following the hand signal and getting the behavior correct 95% of the time, you can add the verbal cue. Say the verbal cue ONCE. Your dog will do one of two things:

- He will respond to your verbal cue and do as you've asked since this is the most recent behavior he's learned! Or in other words, he guessed correctly.

- He will stare at you with a curious look. What does that word mean?

In the first scenario, click and treat that behavior. In the second scenario, use your hand signal to show him what that word means. Once he does the behavior correctly, click and treat him. If for some reason the hand signal does not work, you can always go back to kindergarten and use the food lure to help him get the behavior correct.

All three steps happen on their own. You want to avoid telling the dog to sit while using your hand signal at the same time. If you do so, the dog may only learn the hand signal and not the verbal cue. Dogs communicate through body language and have a preference to watch their environment for cues. Using L.A.W. also prevents us from repeating the same cue over and over without success. If your dog doesn't respond to a verbal cue, show him what you want.

Teaching your dog life skills

It's time to teach your dog what he can do instead of the problematic behavior. The goal is to reinforce the new behavior many, many times so he develops a new behavioral habit. I have a few favorite games and cues that help dogs choose different and healthy behavioral responses.

Stuff a Dog - creating positive associations!

We already discussed how feeding and assuring a dog when they are scared or feeling threatened by a stimulus will not reinforce their reaction. In that case, let's play Stuff-a-Dog. Pair the presence of the stimulus with yummy treats. Deliver them one after another. This technique helps the dog change their association to the sight of the stimulus while also preventing the problematic behavior. It's a great behavior to start with since it's an easy exercise for both you and the dog.

Find it - refocus tool

This is one of my favorite games! When a dog is concerned about her environment, you interrupt that concern with the cue "Find it," and then toss treats on the floor away from the scary stimulus. It's similar to Stuff-A-Dog but instead of feeding directly to the dog's mouth, you are delivering the food on the ground. Benefits include:

- Refocusing your dog's attention to the ground which helps him engage in a coping behavior (sniffing).
- Getting your dog's body moving away from the stimulus.
- Reminding you to do something else instead of tense up and tighten on the leash.
- Creating a positive association with the stimulus since you play the game every time it appears.

- It's one of the easier behaviors your dog can do in the face of something scary.

Touch - refocus tool

Touch is a great way to ask a dog to move in space. I extend my flat palm near the dog's face and when she touches my palm with her nose, I click and treat. I can make the game even harder by moving my hand around in space to add movement into the game. I use touch to refocus my dog away from something in the environment, to get him in and out of the car, and to have him check in with me on off-leash trails.

U-turn - refocus tool

This cue asks the dog to turn away from a stimulus or trigger in the environment. Toss a treat on the ground. Right after your dog finishes gobbling up the treat, cue them to "Turn." When he looks in your direction, click, and jog backward to invite him to chase you. Once he reaches you, deliver the treat. This teaches your dog that removing himself from the stimulus is a better choice. Plus, it's a fun game that gets both of you moving.

Treat and Retreat - for fearful pups

I play this game with fearful dogs all the time. I toss a treat away from me (the scary stimulus), and the dog moves away from me to get it. When he takes a step closer to me, to see if I have any more goodies, I click the movement towards me and then toss the treat away from me. I deliver the treat away from me so the dog does not feel threatened or baited into socializing with me. This technique, of rewarding food and space away from a scary stimulus, has worked time and time again with both my clients' dogs and with countless shelter dogs. They warm up quickly since they have the choice to move away and still get the treat they desire.

Capturing Attention - life skill 101

I start off teaching this behavior indoors to ensure success. Have your dog on a leash, the clicker in hand and some yummy treats. Allow your dog to investigate the environment. When they look back at you, click and treat that behavior. Practice this in the home with a variety of distractions present before moving the game outside on leash. This game teaches the dog that checking in with you despite the distractions is worth their while.

Consistent Communication - life skill 101

I encourage pet parents to stay in communication throughout the entire walk or off-leash experience instead of only communicating when they need something from the dog. Proactive vs. reactive. When I am walking with Sully, I am constantly communicating with him so I stay relevant. I do this by:

• Reinforcing him for offered choices he makes on his own.

• Being playful in my tone and body language, praising him along the way.

• Training when no distractions are present.

• If he is successful, then training when some distractions are present.

This process encourages him to check in with me more often, which comes in handy when I truly need it.

Relax on a Mat

Nan Arthur and Karen Overall both have protocols designed to help your dog relax on a mat despite the distractions present. This skill is not about teaching your dog to "stay" on the mat, rather it's about teaching your dog how to relax in a specific location, the mat. The instructions can be found in Nan Arthur's book *Chill Out Fido!: How to Calm Your Dog*.

For more comprehensive descriptions on how to teach specific life skills and address specific behavior concerns, please check out these additional resources:

Books:

• *Perfect Puppy in Seven Days*, Dr. Sophia Yin

• *Juvenile Delinquent Dogs: The Complete Guide to Saving Your Sanity and Successfully Living with your Adolescent Dog*, Sue Brown

• *Feisty Fido: Help for the Leash Reactive Dog*, Patricia McConnell, and Karen London

- *Fired Up, Frantic, and Freaked Out: Training the Crazy Dog from Over the Top to Under Control*, Laura VanArendonk Baugh

- *Control Unleashed, Creating a Focused and Confident Dog*, Leslie, McDevitt

Online Resources:
- K9 of Mine Website

- Journey Dog Training Blog

- Kikopup YouTube channel

- Domesticated Manners YouTube channel

- Donna Hill YouTube channel

- Eileen and Dogs YouTube channel

◆ Get curious with your dog

- What behavior(s) do you want your dog to do instead of the undesired behavior?

- Which technique(s) will you try to achieve this behavior?

    - Shaping, luring, or capturing

- Where will you practice this behavior so you and your dog are successful?

- What rewards will you use? Remember to use high-value rewards, such as cheese, hot dog, deli meat and boiled chicken.

- When will you increase the criteria?

- How often will you practice this training?

Designing successful training sessions

Now that you have your reinforcers, training techniques and chosen life skills, let's make sure to set up your training sessions for success.

1. Train under threshold.

I sound like a broken record but it's such a common mistake that people make all the time. When your dog is feeling stressed, anxious or fearful, that is not the right time to teach them new skills. So, instead, make sure the environment is positive and safe. If your dog communicates that the environment is not safe by reacting or ignoring you and the training process, either change something about the environment or stop the session and determine a new context in which to train.

2. Easy wins.

Start off your training sessions by asking your dog an easy behavior that he or she knows well to get them invested in the training process. Once your dog is eager and willing to participate in the learning process, then start to make the process a bit more challenging.

You can also implement this strategy during a training session. For example, let's say I want to increase how long Sully can do a down stay behavior. He is successfully staying in position for 10 seconds. I decide to push my criteria and wait for 20 seconds. He gets up from his position. I ask him to lie back down and wait for 3 seconds, in other words, I give him an easy win to get him back in the training game. He waits for 3 seconds, I click and treat. I take note that jumping from 10 seconds to 20 seconds is too hard and decide to gradually work my way up to 20 seconds to ensure success.

3. Payday!

Make sure to keep your rate of reinforcement, how fast you're paying off your learner, high and consistent. A few reasons your rate might dip include the dog is having a hard time understanding what you want or there are too many distractions present. If your dog is not getting the behavior correct, especially in the beginning phase of learning, it's not the dog's problem, it's the trainer's problem. Troubleshoot and make the situation easier for the dog. Ask for a five-foot recall instead of a ten-foot recall.

4. Increase difficulty in small increments.

Most pet parents teach their dog how to come in the living room and then jump straight to asking the dog for an off-leash recall behavior in the dog park. It's like asking a Kindergartener to head into a Ph.D. program. Not going to happen! Break the behavior down in increments.

• Calling the dog to come in the house.

- In the backyard 5 feet away from you, off-leash, no distractions present.

- In the backyard 10 feet away from you, off-leash, no distractions present.

- In the backyard 15 feet away from you, off-leash, no distractions present.

- In the backyard 5 feet away from you, off-leash, distraction present.

- In the backyard 10 feet away from you, off-leash, distraction present.

- In the backyard 15 feet away from you, off-leash, distraction present.

- In the backyard 5 feet away from you, off-leash, new distraction present.

Look at all the work we're doing in the backyard before we even start to change locations. Make sure your dog is getting the behavior correct 95% of the time before increasing the difficulty.

5. Generalize locations.

As mentioned in chapter five, dogs do not have the capability of generalizing a behavior from one context to the next. For example, just because you teach your dog to sit in the living room without distractions present does not mean they know to sit when people come to the door! You need to train that behavior in all contexts to help your dog generalize the behavior.

6. Take breaks and keep it positive!

When teaching something new we want to set up the environment so that the learner is successful and one way to do that is to keep the training sessions short, around 5 minutes. That is a rough time frame as there are some dogs that need shorter time frames and others that could train much longer - border collies, showing off! Just make sure that your dog is successful and that you are both having fun. If not, take a break and re-evaluate the situation before training again.

7. Be realistic and track progress.

I understand that most people did not get a dog to become a dog trainer. They got a dog to experience companionship, friendship, go on adventures and have hair all over the house! However, it must be understood that dog training techniques take time to learn for both the dog and the pet parent. You do not lose weight overnight after working with a personal trainer once.

You do not get over your fear of commitment after one therapy session. And you do not resolve an injury after one physical therapy session. It takes practice, commitment and motivation to find a new way of doing things for both you AND your dog!

I like tracking progress by creating a scoring system. This allows my clients to objectively report on their dog's behavior. We use a Likert Scale and customize it to their dog's behavior, such as 1= least fearful (loose body posture, approaches people) and 5 = most fearful (tense body posture, low growling, backed into a corner). I have the pet parents track their dog's reactions daily so we can collect data and make educated decisions about the training progress.

8. Don't take it personally
This concept can be hard to digest. If the dog is not doing what we expect or desire, we often take that personally and may sometimes even sabotage the relationship. We usually get upset for many reasons.

- We feel disappointed, ashamed, frustrated or impatient because we have unrealistic expectations of our dogs.

- We are upset with ourselves for not practicing the training plan, so we inadvertently take it out on our dogs.

- We have a hard time slowing down in life and expect immediate results in many situations that have nothing to do with training. Unfortunately, this gets translated and projected onto our dogs in the form of timelines and pressure.

Humans and dogs both struggle emotionally at times. The best medicine for this is compassion, patience, and curiosity.

I'm here to tell you that the dog's behavior is not about us. They are not sitting at home, plotting against us. How can I disconnect from him today and make him frustrated?! It's about the dog and his relationship with his environment. With this said, you can stop taking the dog's behavior personally, which will allow you to show up and be more compassionate. Having compassion and patience for your dog during these times is so important for the training process as well as for your relationship. This is an amazing skill to practice with your dog that you can then generalize to all relationships.

Power of habit

I was encouraged to read the Power of Habit by Charles Duhigg. It discusses many of the same topics we talked about in this chapter, applied to humans. When I read the book, I embarrassingly had an epiphany. I can use the behavior modification process for dogs with myself and others. One of the many takeaways from the book includes creating environmental cues for ourselves in order to get a new, desired behavior. For example, if I want to start an early morning stretching routine, I might lay out my yoga mat in the middle of my office floor so I engage in the behavior. I could then reinforce the stretching behavior with a yummy cup of coffee. Simple, right?

✳ Get curious with yourself

- Is there a behavior you engage in that you'd like to modify?

- What would you like to do instead?

- How will you remember to make a different behavior choice?

- How will you reward yourself?

- How will you track your progress?

- Who will hold you accountable?

Chapter 7 References:

- Pryor, Karen. (1999) Don't shoot the dog!: The new art of teaching and training. New York: Bantam Books.

- Sdao, Kathy. (2012) Plenty in Life is Free: Reflections on Dogs, Training and Finding Grace. Wenatchee, Washington: Dogwise Publishing.

- Overall, Karen L. (1997) Clinical Behavioral Medicine for Small Animals. St. Louis, Missouri: Mosby, Inc.

- McDevitt, Leslie. (2007) Control Unleashed: Creating a Focused and Confident Dog. SouthHadley, MA: Clear Run Productions LLC.

- Duhigg, Charles. (2012) The Power Of Habit: Why We Do What We Do In Life And Business. New York : Random House.

CHAPTER 8
Introducing the Six Relationship-Building Principles

In this section of the book, I am going to walk you through the six relationship-building principles. I will discuss what they are, how they show up and ways to achieve them in your relationship with your dog, yourself and others. They include:

• Curiosity

• Acceptance

• Compassionate Communication

• Support & Co-creation

• Trust

• Celebration

In the introduction, I introduced the concept of vulnerability and invited you to be honest with yourself throughout the process of this book. Geraldine Piorkowski, Ph.D., author of *Too Close for Comfort: Exploring the Risks of Intimacy* states that vulnerability can be hard since we run the risk of having our deepest desires trampled upon, rejected, or unfulfilled. However, if we do not get curious with ourselves, then we also run the risk of moving through life without clarity and awareness (Piorkowski, 1994).

When working with pet parents, I encourage them to look at their expectations and possible limiting beliefs they might be projecting onto the dog. These may include:

- Unrealistic expectations: Assuming the dog can do the behavior when they are not ready.

- Negativity bias: Only focusing on the negative behaviors your dog is doing without noticing the positive choices he or she is making.

- Using should statements: Projecting what you think your dog should be like instead of noticing who they are.

- Labeling: Looking at your dog through the lens of a label, which may not take into account all sides of your dog, both positive and negative.

- Emotional redirection or projection: Not being aware of how your emotions are impacting your dog's behavior.

Work on you first

Notice the above limiting beliefs have nothing to do with our dogs or their behavior. They have everything to do with us, bringing awareness to how we're showing up in relationship with our dogs. Byron Katie, speaker, and author, suggests that all of our suffering comes from within, usually stemming from stories and assumptions we have made, most of which are inaccurate. When we believe these inaccurate assumptions, that determines our response or behavior towards the other party, in this case, our dogs. This has the potential to strain the relationship unnecessarily. Katie encourages us to take responsibility for everything in our lives. Once we identify our role and our possible projections, we are empowered to create solutions with an open and curious mind (Katie, 2002).

Designing your relationship alliance

A few weeks after I started my role as the Behavior Manager at the Dumb Friends League, I met with my staff individually and asked them each to design a communication alliance with me. The alliance was meant to be a code of conduct or social promise to one another in regard to our communication. Before I met with the staff individually, I sat down to examine who I wanted to be in relationship with each of them and how I wanted to support them as their leader. I also designed questions to get to know their needs and wants. For example, I asked them how they felt valued, what was the most effective way to communicate with them and how I could deliver constructive feedback, among other questions. We checked in every quarter to determine if any of the agreed-upon topics needed adjustment and to celebrate our communication achievements. I share this with you since I think this practice could be used when examining who you want to be in relationship with your dog and others.

❊ Get curious with yourself

• When do you feel most connected to your dog?

• When and how do you support your dog? How does your dog support you?

• What part of your relationship is worth celebrating and why?

• What will you do when you get frustrated with your dog?

• How will you know when you get stuck in a pattern that doesn't work for both of you?

• What part of your relationship needs improvement and why?

1. Curiosity

Let's rewind to the day I realized Sully's barking and lunging behavior toward dogs was increasing. I remember being overwhelmed and upset, emotions my clients report feeling when they make the phone call to me for help. It took a few deep breaths and a bucketload of compassion to ask myself what was going on. Instead of making Sully or myself wrong, I practiced curiosity and wondered:

• Why is Sully having a hard time?

• What about this situation is making him upset?

• Am I doing anything to help or harm the situation?

I took the time to cultivate both awareness and curiosity about the situation rather than blaming or panicking.

Gaining awareness

Getting curious, my favorite relationship skill, helps everyone gain awareness and clarity. The benefits of getting curious include increased compassion and empathy for your dog, yourself and others. Compassion is defined as concern for the sufferings or misfortunes of others and empathy is defined as the ability to understand and share the feelings of another. I have compassion for Sully when I notice that he is getting stressed by his environment. I am concerned about his well-being; therefore, I modify his experience to help him relax. I also have empathy for him at that moment, as I can relate to feeling uncomfortable or overwhelmed by my environment at times.

These skills come in handy when the behavior modification process is not going the way you expected. For example, imagine your training goal is to ask your dog to check in with you when other dogs walk past her. One day during your training session you notice she is not paying attention to you. She appears stressed, not checking in with you and scanning her environment. As you take a moment to try and understand what could be throwing her off, you notice the construction on the street and realize a number of dogs have passed by. Wow - that is a lot of distraction! She is even starting to show signs of stress, pacing and panting, as the construction noise gets louder. Instead of becoming frustrated, you tune into your compassion and get curious. You decide to move to a quieter street so that she can recover from the situation before you resume training. She's much more successful. Awesome work!

As discussed in chapter one, people often make automatic assumptions about many things in life, especially their dog's behavior. If your dog pees on the carpet when you leave him alone, you might think he is mad at you and is doing so out of spite since you left him home alone. You might become angry at your dog, as he is ruining the carpet. This assumption creates distance between you and your dog, resulting in hard feelings.

There might be other reasons for this behavior concern. Maybe your dog is drinking too much water when you are gone and therefore needs to use the bathroom more often. Or perhaps he realizes that when you are not around he can go to the bathroom without interruption. Or possibly your dog has a urinary tract infection. Instead of getting upset, mind reading, and jumping to conclusions, I invite you to ask questions.

Get curious and try to understand the situation from your dog's perspective.

◆ Get curious with your dog

Curiosity is defined as a strong desire to know or learn. When working with your dog, yourself and others, I define curiosity as asking unassuming questions in order to gain clarity. Unassuming does not mean loaded. When asking questions, you should be open to the answers and not have a specific outcome in mind. You are not asking questions to prove your point, rather to see life from a different perspective, finding the value embedded in the answer.

It was critical to teach you concepts such as, how dogs learn, how they react to stress and the principles of the training and behavior modification process so that you are equipped with the right information to ask the best questions. Being prepared with this information allows you to understand the world from your dog's perspective.

Examples of curiosity questions include:

• Why is my dog having a hard time?

• Am I asking too much from my dog at this moment?

• Is there anything I can do to shift the environment?

• What about this situation is making my dog upset (fill in the blank emotion based on your body language observations)?

• What can I learn from this experience in order to support my dog?

• What is the opportunity here?

✳ Get curious with yourself

Now that you asked yourself questions about your dog and the context, let's go a step deeper and get curious about your emotional reaction to your dog's behavior. When there is a behavior concern present, it can stir up a lot of strong emotions within pet parents. Many people report feelings of embarrassment, shame, frustration, betrayal and overwhelm, to name a few.

These are normal feelings that may come up with anyone or anything in your life, even with your four-legged best friend. It's helpful to pause, notice these feelings, and get curious about yourself. If you do not, you run the risk of operating from these emotions which can negatively impact not only your relationship with your dog but also their behavior.

Examples of curiosity questions include:

• Why am I embarrassed, overwhelmed, or frustrated by this behavior?

• Is my reaction to the situation making the problem worse?

- What part of this situation can I accept in order to take responsibility and make the necessary shift to support both myself and the dog?

- How can I change the situation to relieve stress for both my dog and myself?

✻ Get curious with others

Developing awareness and curiosity is a skill that can absolutely help you in all relationships. Getting curious with others may include understanding life from another person's perspective, asking questions and getting clear on what they might need and where they are coming from. This skill requires self-awareness, noticing the things that trigger you emotionally and then taking the time to check in with the other person involved without assumption.

Examples of curiosity questions include:

- Why am I feeling this way towards this person, thing, or situation?

- Is the story I am telling myself 100% true?

- What else is true about this situation that I might be missing or avoiding?

- Where might the other person be coming from?

- Am I projecting my feelings onto someone else or the situation?

- What is the opportunity in this situation?

- Where do I go from here?

2. Acceptance

It's cold, windy, and snowing outside. You need to take your dog for a walk, not only to provide bathroom relief but also to give your young terrier mix some exercise before he chews up the living room couch. A strong sense of dread washes over you; the last thing you want to do is grab the leash. Looking outside, you groan as you watch the snow pummel down. This, my friends, is resistance: a heavy, wild force that can paralyze people in their tracks. Yikes!

However, you decide that today the horrible weather won't stop you! Shifting your perspective, you pull on your warmest clothes, call your dog over, leash him up, and then head to the door. This is acceptance, an even wilder force that can awaken all possibilities. Yes!

Acceptance and resistance are like houseguests. Sometimes they crash your place at the same time and fight over the last bowl of cereal or who gets to sleep in the spare bedroom. The tension between them can be uncomfortable, to say the least.

Other times only one of them shows up. Resistance usually storms into your home uninvited, tosses his shoes on the floor and overstays his welcome. Ugh! Acceptance, on the other hand, tends to walk in politely bearing fresh flowers and offers to cook a homemade meal. You love it when acceptance shows up!

Why are we talking about resistance and acceptance?
Most of the time it is resistance that prevents people from making a change in their dog's behavior. They might have resistance to the process, for example, not enough time or resources to do the necessary training. Or they might have resistance toward a specific behavior concern, for example, not believing their dog's behavior is getting worse or simply hoping that the dog will grow out of it. In this section, we will explore how we can move away from resistance and lean into acceptance.

Accepting a behavior concern allows us to address it more rapidly.

Providing learning lessons

Accepting difficult behavior or circumstances teaches us to shift our perspective and look for the learning lesson in each experience. My dog Sully likes to take his time on walks, needing to stop and smell everything!! Of course, he does; he is a dog! When I am in a rush, I tend to resist his behavior and get frustrated. The walk becomes tense for both of us. Sully senses my tension and usually slows down even more.

As I thought about this interaction, I realized I wanted to shift my perspective. I wondered, why is this happening and what am I supposed to learn from it? Instead of dreading our walks, I decided I was going to accept however Sully showed up on any given day. After I made this shift, I noticed I was less stressed, more observant and much more content on our walks. Sully responded to my energy by checking in with me more often. We walked together instead of resisting one another. I understood that by slowing down and accepting the situation, I was happier and more present.

Accepting your dog

Learning to accept your dog's behavior can also help relieve some of the shame you might be experiencing. In the past, Sully reacted to the sight of other dogs by barking and lunging when he was on the leash. For so many years, I felt shame about this - I'm a dog trainer, after all! I was hard on myself, not allowing space for self-compassion. The shame grew and it was not long before I started to project my shame onto Sully. If he responded poorly to his environment, I would get frustrated and upset with him. Then I got mad at myself for not taking the time to train him. It was a miserable cycle.

Instead of blaming Sully and myself for our situation, I decided to do a few things:

1. I noticed the resistance.
2. Gave myself permission to experience the sadness that came up for me regarding the situation.
3. Got curious about the context, my role and how to support us moving forward.
4. Reframed the situation as an opportunity.

This exercise allowed me to move from shame and resistance to acceptance and positivity. I felt lighter about Sully, myself and especially our relationship.

My clients talk about this sensation I am referring to as embarrassment. They might be embarrassed that their dog is barking on leash, that he is ignoring their cues in public and that he's humping another dog at the park. I understand why they feel that way. There is a ton of societal pressure for dogs to be perfect all the time. It's unfair to our dogs. We already ask so much of them as it is and now they need to be perfect!? Behavior is fluid and can change at any given moment depending on the circumstance. The sooner we accept that the more loving and compassionate our relationship will become.

Practice "Yes and...."

Practicing acceptance does not mean you cannot take action. You can choose to accept your dog's behavior and also decide to make a change. In the four-step process above, I chose to reframe the situation as an opportunity, a skill I learned through my courses at the Coaches Training Institute.

- "Yes, I am frustrated because my dog is barking on leash, AND I choose to accept it and get the help we need."

- "Yes, I am disappointed in myself for not teaching my dog important life skills, AND I promise to support this process now."

The skill makes room for all perspectives and points of view. It does not make things black or white; it makes room for the gray. You can accept where you are AND make the change.

Get curious with your dog

It's time to learn more about your feelings of resistance regarding your dog's behavior concern.

• Which of your dog's behaviors do you resist?

• How does this resistance impact your relationship with your dog?

• How can you lean into the four-step process the next time you feel resistance?

> • Notice the resistance.

> • Give space for the emotions that come up.

> • Get curious about the resistance. What can you control or change? What do you need to accept as is?

> • Reframe the situation as an opportunity.

Accepting others

Acceptance is a powerful tool. It allows space for everything in your life - the lovely parts and the not so lovely parts. It's easy to accept things when they are beautiful, great and exactly what you want. However, the real growth comes when you accept the challenges that arise and choose to learn and blossom from these experiences.

Get curious with yourself

• Name a time when you did accept something hard in your life.

• What did that look like?

• Who or what helped you through that time?

• What skills did you use to lean into acceptance?

- Describe a situation in your life where you would like to move from resistance to acceptance.

- What is one measurable step you can take towards acceptance in your personal life?

3. Compassionate Communication

A few years ago, a client called me to discuss her dog's behavior. Based on the intake form and my initial consult I determined her dog was "reactive" towards other dogs. Reactive is a term for a dog that barks, growls and/or lunges while on leash. When I used this word to describe the dog, my client stopped me. She suggested we find another, more loving word to describe her dog. I was floored. I loved that idea!

I realized I had made the mistake of labeling this dog using one adjective to describe her whole identity. She was not a "reactive dog"; rather, she was a dog that chose a behavior that worked for her (barking) when dogs got within 10 feet of her on walks. I began to consider the ramifications of labeling and this limited thinking.

Once we narrowly define someone (or some dog), we tend to interpret all his or her behavior under the umbrella of the given label. As a result, we often miss other choices and behaviors the person or dog is making. This is often referred to as negativity bias, introduced by psychologists Paul Rozin and Edward Royzman in 2001. A majority of their work suggested that negative and positive events are not equally salient. We put more emphasis on negative events in comparison to positive events. Their work also suggested that if we notice negative traits about a person or situation, then we will assume the whole is more negative than the sum of its parts (Rozin; Royzman, 2001).

In this case, the client and I changed our language to be more compassionate, by taking into consideration the whole dog and not just the label.

• We practiced narrating all the different body parts and postures to expand our vocabulary so we were specific when describing our experiences and observations.

• Instead of labeling the dog as reactive, we decided to describe the behaviors we observed and the context in which we experienced these behaviors. In other words, we got clear and specific instead of making generalizations about the behavior. If we were to use a label since it's hard to get away from that habit entirely, we would say, "I noticed she is avoidant and by that I mean, she continues to look away from the other dog and remove herself from the situation."

- We chose to notice all the great choices the dog was already making, even without training. When you start paying attention to these choices instead of waiting for the dog to react, you will be amazed at all the behaviors you can start marking and rewarding!

- And, lastly, we chose to celebrate the progress the dog and the pet parent made through the behavior modification process.

Compassionate communication with your dog

Compassionate communication involves noticing the lens that we're using when talking about and to our dogs, getting curious if that language is accurate and offering the dog the benefit of the doubt. A few other examples of labels and language that get in our way include:

- He **never** listens to me.

- He **always** barks.

- He **is** stubborn, dominant, reactive, fill in the blank negative descriptor.

- She **thinks** she needs to retaliate after we left her home alone and that is why she is chewing the couch.

Never and always = These descriptors keep us trapped in our thinking. They do not allow us to see the times when our dog does choose to listen or stops barking since our story (language) proclaims otherwise.

Is = Your dog can be and respond to situations in a variety of ways. When we start to label them as one descriptor, my dog is reactive, dominant or pushy, that is all we'll be able to see. It also prevents us from taking action. Once we believe our dog is something, then we might not develop a plan to support the modification of that behavior. Instead, look at the situation through the ABC lens:

- Antecedent = stimuli, events or conditions that cue the dog to perform a behavior

- Behavior = the response from the dog

- Consequence = the response from the environment that takes place after the behavior has occurred. The consequence determines if the dog's behavior increases or decreases.

Thinks = We do not know what your dog is thinking. All we know is what their body language is communicating to us. Based on these observations, we can infer what they might be feeling but we never truly know what they are thinking.

Being aware of this human tendency can allow us to show up differently and support the behavior process. Our behavior response always plays a role in our dog's behavior response. Noticing what we're thinking and how we are feeling about a situation can help us choose the right behavior in order to support the learning process for our dogs.

◆ Get curious with your dog

- What labels do you use to describe your dog?

- Does this language prohibit you from noticing the positive behaviors and choices that your dog is making?

- What words can you use instead?

Compassionate communication with yourself

After the session with my client, I decided to explore the labels I was using in my own life. The opportunity presented itself in a yoga class. We were in down dog (fitting, right?) after a grueling sequence, when my body started to fatigue. Despite my internal critic, I decided to go into child's pose to relax and give my body a rest. As I knelt into the pose, I heard the teacher invite others to do the same. She said, "If you decide to go into child's pose, it does not become your identity. You are not a slacker. You are not lazy. Rather at this moment, your body is tired and you need a rest."

Mind blown! I loved what she said, and from the sound of the class giggling, so did others. She had given us permission to relax and to avoid labeling ourselves based on one moment in time. Based on this experience, I decided that my identity is not based on single moments or individual aspects of my personality. I can embrace ALL of me.

There are parts of Sully that can be reactive to his environment, but that is not his entire identity! Unfortunately, there was a time where I failed to see this. I told others, "I have a reactive black lab mix." And the more concrete this label became in my mind, the more he and I lived into this way of being, consciously or subconsciously. Two things were probably at play during our walks. To start with, I was worried and expected his reactive behavior; therefore, he sensed my tension and acted accordingly. The second was the more reactive he became the more I focused on those behaviors. This made it nearly impossible to notice when he made different choices such as choosing not to bark and check in with me.

After the experience with my client and the mind-blowing yoga class, I made a promise to Sully - and to myself - that I would stop labeling! I would embrace ALL of our qualities. Sully became my large, black lab mix with a goofy personality who tries his best and I became a strong woman who sometimes needs to rest in child's pose from time to time!

Compassionate communication with others

It's time to use these skills in your personal life. Putting on a new lens and changing your language, allows you to see more in your environment, yourself and other relationships. Try it on and see what shows up!

❋ Get curious with yourself

• Is there someone in your life that you are labeling?

• Do you have a limiting belief about that person?

• Is that perspective 100% accurate?

- What is the opposite of the label you are using? For example, I might be upset with a friend and state my frustration by saying "She never calls me back." I could switch the language to "She tries her best to connect with me." Now I have a new lens to look at her through. Try that lens on and report what's different!

4. Support & Co-creation

Growing up on the east coast, I had never been exposed to the great outdoors. I grew up in dance studios, performing on stages and chasing dance competitions. When I moved to California in 2007, someone invited me on a hike. I thought, "Isn't that just a walk?" Interested, I hopped in the car and we made our way to the Marin Headlands. Walking up the steep incline, watching Sully romp off-leash and admiring the lush vegetation, I thought to myself, "Wow, this is definitely not just a walk."

Fast forward to today and I cannot live without my time in nature. And neither can Sully. Fortunately, when I adopted Sully, I was aware enough to know that I really desired a dog that would accompany me on these nature outings. I loved nothing more than to watch dogs explore the surroundings through their nose, run off-leash and sleep soundly after a long day of hard work!

This is where I feel most connected to Sully. I offer him an opportunity to engage in something he loves to do, while also taking care of myself emotionally and physically. It's crucial for relationships to include support and co-creation, inspiring teamwork, honoring the needs of both parties as individuals and as a unit. Meeting the needs of our dogs not only provide a healthy foundation and hopefully prevent unwanted behaviors, but it can also offer opportunities for connection.

◆ Get curious with your dog

- What activities do you engage in with your dog that you both enjoy?
- How do these activities support your relationship?
- Is there something more you might want from this relationship? If so, how can you make that adjustment?

Support & co-create with your dog

A wise mentor of mine used to say, "We decided to domesticate dogs many, many years ago when they had jobs, fought for survival and had to fend for themselves and their young. Today's dog is expected to grab the remote control, sit on the couch, and watch the latest reruns while we're at work!" Mental stimulation and enrichment activities are vital for every dog, no matter the age. Incorporating enrichment into your dog's daily life is beneficial for a variety of reasons.

- Enrichment provides an outlet for your dog to engage in species-specific behavior.

- It provides mental stimulation and problem-solving opportunities for your dog.

- Since enrichment aims to meet the individual's needs, it can also reduce unwanted behaviors, such as destruction and chewing.

Physical Exercise - Challenging hiking trails, neighborhood walks or runs, and decompression walks (where the dog is allowed freedom of movement in nature) are all great ways to provide physical outlets for your dogs. They get both physical and mental stimulation through exercise and scent.

Play and Games - As we age and take on more responsibility in life, the child in us may forget how to play. Play is a healthy, mindful activity that keeps us young, spirited and engaged. Sully has taught me how to play again, and whenever we go for a walk I make sure we play chase and toss a toy around. We also play hide and go seek inside the house. Other fun games to play include tug of war, fetch and using the flirt pole.

Social Enrichment - Dogs are social beings. Some, not all, loves to play with other dogs. This can be a great mental, physical and social outlet for your dog. It's also a great way to maintain his or her social skills. Make sure to choose appropriate play partners for your dog. Healthy play consists of dogs taking turns (I chase you and then you chase me), changing activities (chasing for several seconds, taking a break and then jaw wresting), frequent breaks and listening to one another's communication efforts. For more information on healthy canine play, please check out the Shelter Playgroup Alliance YouTube channel.

Training - Dogs love to learn, welcome new challenges and thrive when given tasks. All three of these are accomplished when you teach a new skill. I taught Sully how to clean up his toys and bring me his leash when it's time to go for a walk.

Puzzle Toys - Toss out your dog's food bowl and replace it with a variety of puzzle toys. These toys force your dog to really think about how to get a meal instead of just inhaling it, which is great for mental stimulation as well as digestion. A few examples include the West Paw Toppl (my favorite), Canine Genius, Nina Ottosson puzzles, Busy Buddy, and the Kong Wobbler. Regular household items can easily be used as food puzzles as well. Try empty egg cartons and cereal boxes to start.

Sports - Agility, Competition Obedience, and Nosework are a few fun sports to try with your dog. This is an opportunity to build your relationship and mentally enrich your dog through training. Nosework is a great sport for dogs that cannot be on leash around other dogs since the class is structured with one dog working at a time.

For more information on providing your dog with enrichment, please reference *Canine Enrichment for the Real World: Making it a Part of Your Dog's Daily Life* by Allie Bender and Emily Strong.

◆ Get curious with your dog

What are your dog's daily needs?	Are those needs being met?	If not, what can you adjust in order to meet those needs?

Here is a weekly schedule indicating how to incorporate this into your daily life.

	Mon	Tues	Wed	Thurs	Fri	Sat	Sun
Mental	Hide treats in the house	Kong Wobbler	Treats inside an egg carton	Food puzzle	Scatter food in the yard	West Paw Topple	Treats inside a cereal box
Physical	Scent walk	Playdate	Off leash play	Playdate	Scent walk	Hike	Hike

◆ Get curious with your dog

	Mon	Tues	Wed	Thurs	Fri	Sat	Sun
Mental							
Physical							

Support & co-create with others

Noticing what you need in all relationships can be a challenging task to embrace. Our culture puts a lot of emphasis on independence. Flexing our "request" muscle is not a habit that comes easy for most of us. When I started to flex this muscle, I crashed and burned. When I approached someone to discuss my unmet needs, I would react from a triggered, emotional state. None of my language allowed us to co-create solutions since the person felt backed into a corner. I knew it was important to state my desire but I also needed to create a safe space for the other person.

So I decided to change my language from "I need you to (fill in the blank)" to "I would like to make a request." Wow, did that make a difference for everyone involved. When I changed my language, I was softer and less attached to the outcome which allowed us to discuss the content and co-create solutions.

✺ Get curious with yourself

- What do you need from the relationship with your dog?
- What do you need in other relationships? Are there any parallels between the two?
- Is there someone you need to communicate your needs to?
- What positive impact will this have on your life when you say what you need to say?
- What solutions can you co-create with this person so you can both get what you need?

5. Trust

Trust is a key ingredient in maintaining the health of any relationship. Trust is defined as the firm belief in the reliability, truth, ability, or strength of someone or something. In this section, we will discuss how to develop and maintain trust between you and your dog. Since we cannot ask our dogs if they trust us, we must rely on reading their body language to make sure they feel safe and comfortable with us or the situation.

The right ratio

The Gottman Institute has done a lot of research when it comes to successful marriages. Through their work, they have found that there must be a 5:1 ratio in order to maintain trust and cultivate a healthy relationship. 5 positive interactions to every 1 negative interaction. They define positive interactions as showing interest, asking questions, showing affection and demonstrating that their partner matters to name a few. They define negative interactions as being emotionally dismissive, critical or defensive (Gottman, J.M. & Levenson, R. 1999).

We can assume the same with our dogs. Challenging interactions between us and our dogs will happen. We will disagree, we will get frustrated, we will ask them to do things they do not want to do and vice versa, just like any relationship. However, we want to make sure that we have cultivated more positive experiences than negative experiences so that when something challenging comes up, it does not tip the scales. Dr. Susan Friedman and Steve Martin, refer to this concept as the relationship trust account (Friedman & Martin, 2013).

Making deposits to the relationship trust account:

• Meeting your dog's social, mental, emotional and physical needs.

• Saying no to an on-leash greeting with another person and their dog if your dog is trying to avoid the situation.

• Saying no to a person wanting to greet your fearful dog.

- Making the training process fun and successful.

- Offering your dog the choice to remove himself from a situation.

Making withdrawals from the relationship trust account:

- Not meeting your dog's needs and then blaming them for destructive behavior.

- Restraining the dog to clip their nails despite their attempted efforts to avoid you.

- Getting frustrated and yelling at your dog during the training process.

- Handing off your fearful, squirming puppy so that a stranger can hold them and say hello.

Develop & maintain trust with your dog

Choice is a primary reinforcer for all organisms. Being able to control one's own outcomes can be just as reinforcing, if not more, than food and water (Friedman, 2013). We make choices for our dogs all day long, without asking them to weigh in. Think about it, we choose what to feed them, when they get access to the outdoors or social interactions, and when they need to continue walking and avoid sniffing. This approach leaves little room for collaboration.

In my workshops, I often present this exercise. I ask the audience to close their eyes and visualize this scenario. You are driving to a potluck dinner. You are so excited to engage with friends and family after a long week. On the way to dinner, you get caught in traffic. You reach for your phone and click on Google Maps to look up an alternative route to avoid the traffic. The app is not working. You cannot find an alternative route and now you're stuck moving at a snail's pace, inching down the highway.

At the end of the scenario, I ask the audience to call out how they are feeling in this situation. Most report feeling panicked, out of control, trapped and unsettled. I ask them, "What if the app started working and you were able to take the next exit and find a faster route to the party? How would you feel then?" They usually show signs of relief, smiles resuming on their faces and explain that having control over their route to the party was a much better outcome. This is a silly example; however, the emotional impact between the first scenario and the second is pretty dramatic. Providing our dogs with choice and control over their outcomes can have the same positive effect.

I heard a great trainer on a recent podcast say something so brilliant that applies to all relationships. "If you're not going to like the answer, then don't ask the question." You are not providing choice in a relationship if you are not allowing space for the other person or dog to speak their truth. For example, if I ask my dog to come upstairs from the basement and he chooses not to and I make him do it anyway, just because I asked the question does not mean I am providing choice. If I truly ask the questions, I must be willing to hear all outcomes, not just the one I want to hear.

Ways to offer choice:

• Taking a break during nail clipping when my dog indicates that he is stressed out

• Allowing my dog to exit a social interaction with another dog if he is feeling overwhelmed.

• Proving my dog a variety of mental stimulation puzzles or toys to choose from.

• Following my dog on the walk and letting him explore all the scents instead of dictating the route.

Admittedly, I have run into this many times in my human relationships, asking a question in order to get the answer I want to hear instead of being open to all possibilities. Now that I am aware of this tendency, I try to head into these conversations with a few things in mind:

• Determine what I might need to communicate or ask for.

• Do not ask a question in place of stating my request. That is an unintentional way of avoiding stating my desire.

• Be open and curious about the other person's point of view.

- Remind myself that I may not receive what I am hoping for.

- Be open to compromise and co-creating solutions.

Be your dog's advocate

In chapter two, I told you how I avoid putting Sully into challenging situations in attempts to create positive experiences and build trust between us. However, there used to be a time where I chose social pressure over his needs. In the past, pet parents have asked me if their dog can say hello to Sully. A handful of times, I have ignored Sully's desire to avoid the interaction and pressed forward with the meet and greet. In these situations, I got lucky in the sense that he did not escalate beyond freezing when saying "hello".

Many pet parents put their dogs through these experiences daily. I see it all the time. Their dogs are silently uncomfortable (absence of barking and lunging) with the interaction. Since the dog appears to be "fine" the behavior of the pet parent is reinforced and so the leash greetings commence until one day it's not fine for the dog and then it's his fault for barking and lunging.

It's so important to find your voice and advocate for your dog regardless of what others might say or think. They count on us to keep them safe so determine how you will handle these situations when they arise.

◆ Get curious with your dog

- How can you provide more choices for your dog?

- In what situations do you advocate for your dog?

- In what situations are you not advocating for your dog? How can you support them instead?

Develop & maintain trust with others

I am aware that developing and maintaining trust in human relationships is more complex than solely balancing your experiences and offering choices; however, it's a great place to start. If you're looking for additional ways to develop and maintain trust, turn to the other five relationship-building principles:

- Get **curious** and avoid assumptions. Listen to others in order to gain a new perspective.

- Lean into **acceptance** and away from resistance.

- Communicate with **compassion**. Avoid using labels and all-or-nothing language.

- **Support & co-create** balancing both parties' needs.

- Lastly, you'll learn about this next one soon, **celebrate** the other person, yourself and the relationship.

6. Celebration

"Welcome back to week two of your life skills class. Tonight we are going to review concepts from last week and then we'll cover some new techniques for you to implement with your canine companion. But first, I'd love to hear something positive about your dog's behavior from this past week."

Silence. Crickets. Pin Drop.

One brave soul speaks up and says, "My dog has started to realize that the clicker predicts food. When I bring the clicker out for a training session, he perks up and runs over to me. But he still doesn't listen to me all the time. Just today he refused to...". I gently interrupt the client, reinforce him for noticing that the dog understood the clicker's association and ask him to name a few more positive attributes about the dog.

"Anyone else?"

Silence. Crickets. Pin Drop.

Someone else volunteers, "My dog did a great job sitting when I used the hand signal this week. But he still doesn't sit when I cue it verbally." Yet again, I refocus the client back to the positive part of her statement.

"Next week - and from here on - please be ready to share a "brag" about your dog. Brags are anything positive about your dog's behavior that you notice in between classes. It can be hard to see them in the beginning, but if your dog were perfect you wouldn't be in this class. (Chuckles heard around the room.) Just wait, though! It's amazing how many good behaviors you will begin to observe when you make the conscious effort to notice them."

Celebrate your dog

Celebration! It's one of the most important concepts in this book, in training, and in our lives! Most of us take very little time if any, to stop and smell the roses and celebrate achievements, no matter how big or small they are. And yet, it is crucial! When we are positive about progress, even if the improvements seem to be incremental, the excitement can snowball into big change.

Most of us wait to celebrate an achievement until the very end; however, there are many opportunities along the way worthy of celebration. Here are some examples of celebrating behavior as a work in progress:

- Your dog starts barking at the sight of another dog. You want to interrupt the behavior so you cue him to touch your hand with his nose. He barks a few more times before he can refocus his attention back to you. Before you started the training process, he was unable to listen to anything around him when he noticed a dog, so this is a big win. Click and treat yourselves!

- Your dog is able to come when called while off-leash without other distractions present. Another hiker appears which piques your dog's curiosity. He has a delayed response when you call him to come due to his interest in the hiker; however, he makes his way to you. Celebrate this choice.

- You invite a friend over to introduce to your fearful dog. You are hopeful your friend will be able to connect with your dog, possibly even pet him. You introduce the dog to your friend slowly, watching his body language, making sure to only go at his pace. He sniffs your friend's hand and then backs up and avoids the interaction. Despite your unmet expectations, you celebrate your dog feeling brave enough to investigate the new person and celebrate yourself for not pushing your dog over threshold!

How will you reward your dog for the great choices he or she makes?

- Provide a high-value yummy treat such as freeze-dried liver, a bully stick or frozen marrowbone.

- Take him on his favorite walk or hike.

- Take her swimming.

- Give him a canine massage.

- Schedule a play date with one of her human or canine friends.

- Give extra belly rubs.

- Give her doggy ice cream on a hot day.

- Provide an extra play session.

- Take him for a ride in the car (only if he enjoys that).

Celebrate yourself

And how will you reward yourself? Remember to reward yourself every time you:

- Create, revise, and update training plans.

- Implement new tools and management strategies.

- Foster new habits.

- Focus on the positive choices your dog is making.

- Choose kindness and self-care over frustration.

- Lean into the six relationship-building principles.

Some of my favorite ways to celebrate:

- Eat a piece of chocolate.

- Take time to relax and watch a movie I've been excited about.

- Dance and smile in the mirror.

- Treat myself to a latte.

- Share a success with a friend.

Celebrate others

This concept applies to everyone in your life! Give them positive feedback, right at the moment, if you can. This not only communicates what works for you but it also gives the other person the opportunity to receive great feedback. Who will you celebrate and how will you celebrate them?

Chapter 8 References:

Intro

• Piorkowski, Geraldine. (1994) Too close for comfort: exploring the risks of intimacy. Cambridge, Massachusetts: Perseus Books Group.

• Katie, B., & Mitchell, S. (2002) Loving what is: Four questions that can change your life. New York: Harmony Books.

Curiosity

• Piorkowski, Geraldine. (1994) Too close for comfort: exploring the risks of intimacy. Cambridge, Massachusetts: Perseus Books Group.

• Katie, B., & Mitchell, S. (2002) Loving what is: Four questions that can change your life. New York: Harmony Books.

• Brown, B. (2006). Shame Resilience Theory: A Grounded Theory Study on Women and Shame. Families in society: the journal of contemporary human services, 87(1):43-52.

Compassionate Communication

• Rozin, P. & Royzman, E. (2001). Negativity Bias, Negativity Dominance, and Contagion. Personality and Social Psychology Review, Vol. 5, No. 4, 296–320.

Trust

• Gottman, J.M. and Levenson, R. What predicts change in marital interactions over time? A study of Alternative models. Family Processes Journal. 38.2 (1999). I43-58. Print.

• Friedman, Susan and Martin, Steve. (2013). The Power of Trust. Retrieved from: http://www.behaviorworks.org/files/articles/The%20Power%20of%20Trust.pdf

CHAPTER 9
Conclusion

So now that you've made it to the end of the book, I hope you can see what I have been able to experience through my 12 years experience in animal sheltering, operating my private dog training practice and my relationship with Sully. Our relationship with our canine companions can be a window into how we relate to the world around us. It gives us insight into what holds us back and shows us where we can expand and connect in our own lives.

This lesson has afforded me the opportunity to connect more intimately in my relationship with Sully, my relationship with others and most importantly my relationship with self. I invite you to refer back to your favorite chapters whenever you need reminders to support you and your dog or inquiries to gain clarity. I invite you to understand, accept, and love all parts of your dog, others and yourself.

ABOUT THE AUTHOR

Marissa Martino, CTC, CPDT-KA began her career working with canines after attending the Academy for Dog Trainers in 2007. Since then, Marissa has had the pleasure of working for three different animal shelters directing their behavior departments in CO & CA, the most recent being the Dumb Friends League.

Marissa has implemented many innovative canine and feline behavior modification programs. As a result of these efforts, Marissa was invited to present at the Humane Society of the United States annual conference in 2014 and 2107, Ontario SPCA's annual conference as well as Petfinder's Adoption Option shelter conferences. In addition to that success, Marissa has provided behavior consulting to shelters in Texas, Colorado, California, Puerto Rico, and Hawaii.

Currently, Marissa is working for the Dumb Friends League as their Community Liaison offering consulting, education and resources to shelters and animal welfare professionals in rural Colorado. She is thrilled to be making a difference on a statewide level.

Marissa also operates her private dog training practice, Paws & Reward, in Boulder, CO. Marissa's unique approach inspires behavioral transformation for both dogs and their pet parents. She believes that our relationship with our canine companions can be a window into how we relate to our world around us which allows us an opportunity to expand as individuals. Marissa's innovative, personal development approach is designed to help people cultivate self-awareness and intimacy in the relationship with their dog, themselves and others.

Visit her website to check out her services, online courses, and free resources: pawsandreward.com. Marissa also co-hosts a podcast called Canine Conversations: canineconvos.com.

CPSIA information can be obtained
at www.ICGtesting.com
Printed in the USA
LVHW081544090221
678829LV00043B/1522